THE PRESENT STATE

OF

THE FINE ARTS IN FRANCE

Printed by A. Salmon & Ardail. Paris.

THE PRESENT STATE

OF THE

FINE ARTS IN FRANCE

BY

Philip Gilbert Hamerton

AUTHOR OF 'THE GRAPHIC ARTS,' 'LANDSCAPE,'
&c. &c.

With Many Illustrations

LONDON
SEELEY AND CO. LIMITED
ESSEX STREET, STRAND
1892

CONTENTS

LIST OF ILLUSTRATIONS

PLATES

VIGNETTES

LIST OF ILLUSTRATIONS

PREFACE

ALL the branches of the fine arts have undergone great changes in France during the last twenty-five years, and these changes may usually be attributed to one of two causes—the increased liberty of the artist, and the invasion of the democratic spirit. Some of us are old enough to remember the time when French public opinion allowed very little liberty to artists. They were permitted with great difficulty, and very unwillingly, to do anything that had not been done before, so that every young artist who had anything new or original to express had a very hard battle to fight, and fought it, if he had not private means, at the risk of absolute starvation. One after another, a succession of original men have broken down this narrow-minded opposition, and in the present day, whatever may be the faults of the French school, it cannot be accused either of monotony or of slavish obedience to a narrow-minded public opinion. It is as favourable even as the English to the development of original faculty of all kinds. For instance, with regard to colour, we remember the time when French landscape-painters were not permitted to attempt the full colouring of Nature; they might not copy her greens, her azures, her purples, or her intensities of orange, crimson, and scarlet. They were to confine themselves to the colouring of Claude, which is not unpleasant on the walls of a room, because it is quiet and unobtrusive, but which hardly more represents the strength and variety of nature than if it were simple monochrome. Even Corot, who died recently, conformed to the old French desire for very quiet colouring in landscape, and he never attempted the intensity of southern light. The landscape-painters who worked along with Theodore Rousseau saw more of natural colour, but they did not venture upon full sunshine. I do not mean that they never attempted it, but that they were still sufficiently under the influence of picture galleries to keep something of the old blackness and to colour their shadows on the old principles. At the present day many French artists try boldly both for colour and light, and, although the crudity of some of their attempts has exposed them to ridicule, their influence is extending over the whole school. The desire for fidelity in colour makes each man paint what he sees. If there is any imperfection in his vision, so much the worse for his work; the imperfection will be apparent, and it will not be masked by any conventionalism. M. Rouffet, in his picture of a charge of cavalry falling into a pit at Waterloo (an illustration of Victor Hugo), paints horses a rich purple, and is careful to outline the shadows on the earth with the colours of the rainbow. In a word, his vision is not achromatic. There is another danger in the tendency to see what we think we ought to see. Perhaps in the last century landscape-painters honestly believed that they saw shadows brown, as to-day they honestly think they see them blue, purple, or violet. However this may be, a Frenchman is now free to colour in perfect sincerity, and he did not enjoy this *freedom in the early decades of the present century. The consequence is a glare in the exhibitions quite rivalling that which used to be present in English exhibitions, and which was also due to the unrestricted study of nature. An unforeseen consequence of imitating natural colour is that pictures have almost ceased to be convenient articles of furniture. A Titian harmonises well with any rich furniture and hangings, a Teniers or any old Dutch picture goes well with old oak; but what furniture in the world recalls the colouring of a Monet or a Montenard? The French, in fact, have reached that stage in the differentiation of the art of painting when it has no connexion with the decorative arts,* except when it is intentionally subordinated to decoration. *Even in mural painting they have great difficulty in restricting themselves to the exigencies of architecture. In the mural paintings of the Panthéon, only two artists—Puvis de Chavannes and J. Blanc—have conformed to the requirements of the building, and, of the two, Puvis de Chavannes has done this the more completely; I mean that when the eye, after wandering over the architecture, passes to his wall-painting of the youth and pastoral life of St. Geneviève, it feels no difficult transition from one art to the other. The tones of the painted space are not in contradiction with those of the pavement and the pillars. In work of this kind, nature is almost out of the question. It is enough that the natural colouring be suggested; the chief necessity is that the building shall remain a decorated building, and not be converted into a picture gallery. The* Battle of Tolbiac, *by J. Blanc, is a finely conceived representation of the supernatural interference at that battle, which is said to have converted Clovis; it is poetical in conception and impressive with its heat and dash of onset, and its sheaves of spears, under the guarding Heaven that watches and intervenes. With all this the artist has not forgotten that he is painting for a building of light stone, and that full picturesque chiaroscuro is forbidden to him. His work is decorative, and its colouring is light, though not without energy in its lightness. From that we pass to the* Last Moments of St. Geneviève, *by Laurens. Of all the mature French artists, there is not one more gifted for the serious conception of historical subjects, nor one who has studied more thoroughly the early history of France. His St. Geneviève is touching as a representation of approaching death, and interesting as a glimpse of a barbarous past that had still its own virtues and consolations. Still, it is rather a gallery picture than a piece of mural decoration. Its darks are too vigorous, its lights too bright, its realisation too powerful for wall-painting. The work of M. Maillot in the Panthéon is too much a piece of mediaeval illumination to be a suitable accompaniment for Renaissance architecture. The St. Denis of Bonnat is a strong piece of chiaroscuro—too strong for its place in a building where the wall ought not to be destroyed by illusory distances. M. Lévy and M. Cabanel decided the question for themselves by simply painting large historical pictures from the lives of Charlemagne and St. Louis—pictures in which there is much merit, yet which do not hold well together in a public edifice.*

Such is the result of individual freedom in the Panthéon. In the Mairies aud in the Hôtel de Ville it is much worse. There modern democracy, as well as modern individualism, finds its full expression. Considered by itself, The Vault of Steel, *by M. Laurens, is a work of unquestionable power. It represents the occasion of a visit made by Louis XVI. to the Hôtel de Ville by way of reconciliation with the people. Bailly, the Mayor of Paris, and La Fayette, commander of the National Guard, had wished the King to go to the Hôtel de Ville on the 17th of July, 1789, as a friendly manifestation. The Royal Family had so little confidence, that the Queen and Princes opposed the journey to Paris, and the King himself, before undertaking it, made arrangements for a Regency in case he should not return. Bailly had been to meet the royal carriages at a point half-way between Versailles and Paris, and when the combined procession reached the Hôtel de Ville, Bailly, as Mayor, received his Majesty, and the Councillors made with their swords a vault of steel, under which Louis passed into the building. As he approached, and before he ascended the steps, Bailly handed him the*

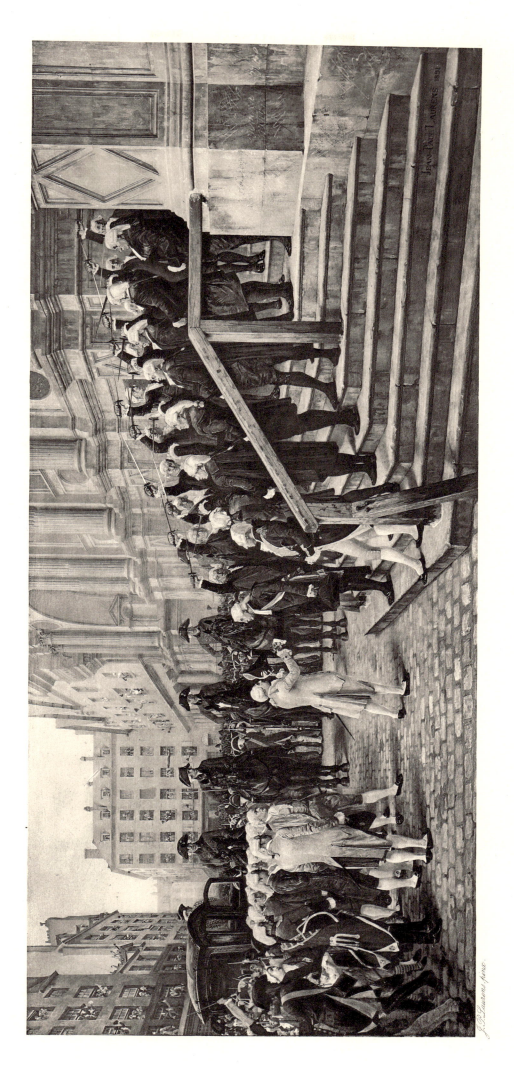

J. P. Laurens, pinxit.

JEAN-PAUL LAURENS. 1838

The Vault of Steel.

Parisian bi-colour, a red and blue cockade, which the King accepted, and which became the tri-colour by the addition of the royal white at the suggestion of La Fayette. The picture is in the best sense historical, as portraits and other documents exist in abundance, and it is also full of character, especially in the figure of Louis XVI., the keen, sallow face of Bailly, and the stalwart form of Lafayette, who is standing on the lowest step in the near foreground.

In the hands of M. Laurens there can be no objection to a revolutionary subject, but in more vulgar hands these subjects easily become tumultuous and unpleasant—interesting, it may be, for a moment in an exhibition, but unsuited to the permanence and continued publicity of wall-painting. Then there is the neighbourhood of other works, often quite unsuited to accompany splendid architecture, and having little to recommend them, except a decided democratic tendency. And even a common democracy of sentiment does not ensure any similarity of artistic conception. For example, a mural picture by M. Gilbert represented a Goods Station, and attracted much attention by the force and vigour with which, on a large scale, the life and work and the encumbering things of a goods station were represented. I need not describe it further: every reader will imagine for himself the locomotive, the drays, the porters, the barrels and hampers, and the rest. What I mention the picture for is that its scheme of colour was chiefly in strong browns, blacks, and greys, almost approaching monochrome. Quite near it were exhibited two other democratic mural pictures by M. Chabas, one of them representing a wedding feast in the lower middle-class, and the other a working-man's family taking a Sunday excursion into the country, or half-country, in the immediate neighbourhood of Paris. Each of these pictures was very consistently conceived as to its colouring, but it was remote from the colouring of Nature, and still farther from the darks of the old masters. Pale greens, pinks, violets, with warm white and a sort of grey to stand for black, with something that suggested flesh-colour without realising it, were the principal elements of this strange, yet, as I have said, consistent colouring. Here we are, indeed, in what to Rembrandt, or even to Reynolds, would have been the art of a most remote and inconceivable future. By themselves works of this class may stand when once their principle is admitted; but woe to them if a strong brown picture, like that of M. Gilbert, were admitted in the same room — and this is what, with the present carelessness about the juxta-position of opposite kinds of art, might not improbably happen. In one important point most of these democratic pictures really do attain striking success — that is, in the observation of human life: they represent the French ouvrier and his wife and family, or the little bourgeois with his household, precisely as they live with each other, and as if nobody of a different class was observing them.

The effect of the democratic tendency on sculpture has been to reduce its dignity whilst increasing its interest and pathos. There is a bronze statue of David, by M. Béguine, purchased by the State, and given to the gallery at Autun. David has just decapitated Goliah, and stands with his great sword before him in the first moment of his triumph. Almost all sculptors who have dealt with this subject hitherto have made David strong, well-built, and as dignified as his years would permit; so one is rather taken aback at first by M. Béguine's David, who is meagre, ill-grown, and inelegant. On further acquaintance, however, the work gains upon us by its extreme veracity, and by the quantity of mind and character that the artist has put into the face and gesture of his young hero. There is more in that bronze lip than in many a handsome statue. These are the strong points of the democratic art of the present day — its observation of facts of all kinds in colour, light, and form; and in the representation of mankind, its keen analysis of character.

I add merely this remark as to the future, that since the vitality of the French school has never been greater than it is now, or its industry more energetic, everything may be hoped for it except progress in delicacy of taste — a quality that many French artists have possessed in perfection, but which in the present day seems to be often neglected for the triumphant display of

*science and power.   I need only mention two names, those of M. Rochegrosse and M. Roll,
both of whom are unquestionably men of great force, which was manifested in M. Rochegrosse
at a very early age.   M. Roll, however, is so versatile, and has so much freshness and variety,
that he may at any time belie the estimates of criticism, and distinguish himself as much by
some unexpected display of taste as he has done already by the most opposite kinds of
characterisation.*

THE PRESENT STATE OF THE
FINE ARTS IN FRANCE

I

The Calm after Worn-out Controversies

IT is more than twenty years since I wrote two little volumes on 'Contemporary French Painters' and 'Painting in France after the Decline of Classicism,' and my first attempt in art criticism was an article for a quarterly review on the Salon of 1863. Since those days events have taken place of such enormous political importance that the movement of the French school might have been greatly perturbed by them; yet it does not appear that either the war which reduced France to a secondary place in Europe, or the revolution which substituted a republic for an empire, prevented the school from following its own natural course of development. The war has been, no doubt, productive of military illustrations, all the more truthful because the artists observed warlike incidents with their own eyes; but as French battles in 1870 were almost exclusively a series of defeats, people do not greatly desire to be reminded of them, and it is only the professed military painters who have dwelt on them very much. The practical effect of the war was to suspend artistic productiveness for a time, and there was lamentable misery amongst the poor or the improvident members of the artistic profession. Then came the Commune, in which a great painter and a great sculptor were implicated; but one of these soon afterwards found rest in the grave, and the other, Dalou, more active than ever, has found refuge from anxiety in success. The principal effect of the war upon the fine arts has been, therefore, simply to increase the veracity of military painting and drawing of all kinds. For example, there are the etchings by Lançon, published under the title 'La Troisième Invasion.' Their author was so strongly impressed by those terrible realities which he had witnessed that he made no attempt to please the eye by elegant artistic arrangements, but drew just what he had seen, giving nothing of art but truth. It happened that when the war broke out there were two military painters of first-rate ability, De Neuville and Detaille, both of whom had powers of observation and of memory far surpassing the average, even amongst artists, and a sense of grace and elegance that was wanting in Lançon. They gave their own record of the war in pictures of incidents, chiefly of combats on a small scale, better within the powers of art than the battle pictures of former times, and there can be no doubt that the works of these artists and their followers will convey to future generations an extremely accurate idea of the military life of 1870.

The revolution of that year and its consequences had less influence on the fine arts than preceding revolutions. It was suddenly accomplished, with few dramatic incidents except those attending upon the flight of the Empress, and although it may fill two or three interesting pages of written history, it is not nearly so attractive to artists as the terrible events of a hundred years ago. The establishment of the Republic has had no influence upon the fine arts of a direct nature except by continuing the usual degree of governmental patronage. The plain costume worn by the President on official occasions and the comparative paucity of display have made the few ceremonial pictures that are still painted less imposing than their predecessors; but pictures of this class count for little comparatively with the immense productiveness of France. The real influence of the Republic on art has been in the preservation of order and peace, and in a sort of friendliness to art which, without being energetic or meddlesome, is still favourable; as, for example, in the annual and universal exhibitions and in the honours awarded to distinguished artists. The truth is that the productivity of the fine arts in France is too vast in the present day for royal patronage to have any appreciable effect upon it, so that the most desirable state of things is simply the independence of artists secured to them by a Government that protects their peace. The direct influence of all French Governments on painting has been more or less unfortunate, by encouraging young men to produce very ambitious historical works, often beyond their mental capacity and without any charm as art. Young painters sometimes make out for themselves a sort of programme for their future career. One of them, who has succeeded, told me twelve years ago that his programme was as follows:—First, to paint very big pictures, to attract attention in the Salon; secondly, to choose his subjects with an eye to purchase by the Government for provincial museums; thirdly, to begin to think about attractive pictures to win customers amongst private lovers of art. In this programme the patronage of the Government intervenes to encourage a young painter in producing a kind of art, often coarse and without charm, for which there is no real demand.

During the last twelve or fifteen years mural painting has been encouraged both by the French Government and by municipal bodies, especially by the Parisian *conseil municipal* and the *arrondissements* of Paris. There has also been a good deal of mural painting for provincial churches, museums, and municipal buildings. Here the intervention of the Government and of other public bodies is much more necessary than in ordering or purchasing gallery pictures, and the result has been in isolated cases entirely satisfactory; but the difficulty is, when several painters are employed upon one building, to give commissions in such wise that the works of different men may, in their association, produce a harmonious whole. For example, in the Pantheon, the architecture is absolutely harmonious, there is not a discordant note; but it was decided to give commissions for mural paintings, and artists of the most opposite character were employed, who have introduced into the building an element of incongruousness that is a distinct injury to its artistic unity. So it is with the noble staircase of the museum at Amiens, admirably decorated, as to the walls, with paintings by Puvis de Chavannes, but spoiled in its unity by a ceiling painted on entirely different principles. The plain fact is that men invested with political or municipal authority very rarely understand painting well enough to employ different talents on the same building. However, if mural painting is to be practised on a scale of any importance it must be through the encouragement of public authorities. The same may be said of sculpture, even more strongly, as there is room for mural painting in some of the larger private houses and cafés, where sculpture, except in the form of statuettes or bas-reliefs, is too much in the way. The present important school of French sculpture exists almost entirely by State patronage. This opens the whole question whether it is right to maintain any fine art without regard to natural supply and demand.

French State patronage maintains ceramic art in the porcelain factory at Sèvres, it supports tapestry-weaving at the Gobelins, and if it did not help to maintain dramatic art at the Théâtre Français it is certain that the most refined and learned French acting could not be long preserved as a tradition of past excellence. I allude to dramatic art merely as an example, for these pages are not the place where its condition might be examined, and the subject lies quite outside of my competence. Mural painting is dependent either on the patronage of the State or upon that of public corporations. Sculpture, on a scale of any importance, would perish without State help, yet it is an art for which many Frenchmen have a remarkable natural aptitude. Now, when the natural aptitude exists, ought the State to encourage it in spite of the absence of a demand? The answer may be that there *is* a demand in the national, though hardly in the personal and individual sense. The Frenchman does not desire to encumber his narrow *appartement* with statues, but he may agree with all his cultured countrymen in thinking it right that the national gift for sculpture should be nationally encouraged. And in a case like that of France, where the gift is so unquestionably real, the excuse for national interference is that, without it, a genuine talent would lie dormant. Here is a case in point. I knew Gautherin, the sculptor, when he was poor, ill, and without reputation; but he was a man of genius, and his genius was strictly that of a sculptor—it never could have found adequate expression in painting. His only hope, in those days, was in Government patronage, and what a wild hope it seemed! He was so poor that he could not afford to pay a workman for even the roughest hewing of his marble: he worked by himself all day, and most of the night too, that he might have a marble statue in the Salon. Well, it was finished in time, and the artist and I were visiting the Salon on successive days together. One morning he came looking so bright and happy that I said, 'Some piece of good luck has happened to you: what is it?' The Government had bought his statue for rather a handsome price—eight hundred pounds if my memory serves me. That sum of money was for Gautherin the possibility of going on with his art in peace, and he cared for nothing else. He died prematurely after all, but not before he had done great things.

If any one asks, 'What is the good?' the answer must be that gifts which exist in the race are worth cultivating. In England there is often a natural aptitude for scholarship, and although ancient Greek is not useful in the vulgar sense, the study of it is encouraged by University endowments. There is also a secondary kind of utility in great studies. The encouragement of sculpture by the French State has indirectly served to maintain a high quality in carving, and classical studies in literature have done something for the better class of English journalism.

The interest of the present condition of French art lies in the definite and complete triumph of modernism or, to imitate the French word, modernity. Neither one nor the other of these words is above criticism, but they are both in use, and it might be difficult to invent a better. One may imagine the objection that as the taste of each epoch is modern whilst it lasts, all the epochs of art must have witnessed the triumph of that which, for the time, was modernism. The objection would be erroneous, in this way: former epochs have been governed by some kind of tradition, but modernism in art is especially marked by liberty of the most complete kind—so complete, indeed, that the modern spirit considers itself free to accept, and free to reject, everything that the past has to offer by way of instruction or example. Observe that in a settled conventional state of things men are not free to reject the past, and in a revolutionary state they are not free to accept it. Modernism has got beyond both these stages; its liberty is much more complete than that of the revolutionist, because it has left revolutions behind. Nobody now calls himself a 'romantic' or a 'realist,' though every one is perfectly free to take what seems good to him in the romance or realism of the past. So there are no professed mediaevalists now, though the Middle Ages are better understood than ever they were before, and in all matters of archaeological detail more faith fully represented. The bigoted and exclusive classical school is now like a dead religion — it is gone, and it cannot be set up again; yet the fruit of classical studies is still visible whenever a Greek or Roman subject is attempted, and a genuine interest is proved by serious endeavours to represent the past as it must have been. The most recent war-cry has been Impressionism, or the doctrine that artists ought to paint ocular rather than material truth, what they see rather than what they know. This, however, is by no means a novelty, as visual suggestion and selection are the principles of all effective sketching. What is some- what new in the commonest impressionist pictures is the audacity with which false relations of colour and tone are presented as superior to the usual methods of criticism, on the ground that whether true to nature or not they are faithful to the artist's impression, the only kind of fidelity which he professes to desire.

The reader sees how convenient this doctrine is as an escape from positive laws of truth. To employ a distinction common in Germany, it makes the truth of painting subjective rather than objective, and the painter can always answer that his brain receives impressions as he represents them. One does not see how the painter, to borrow a common phrase, can be 'brought to book.' It is useless to enter into any controversy with him about his own im- pressions, and if he tells us that his pictures are faithful to these, he may claim to be the best authority. The only criticism to which a professed impressionist is amenable is the simple statement of dislike. We can say, 'No doubt your impression has been faithfully rendered, as you say so, and therefore the picture may be interesting to yourself as a record of mental experience, but it does not concern us.' An impressionist would thus be left with a collection of works of a private and personal value, but no more. It may, however, be doubted whether fidelity to the impression has always the completeness that is claimed for it. For example, the principle of work from nature, advocated by Georges Michel, that the artist ought to stop short when the effect changes, would be excellent if he could produce harmonies of colour as rapidly as Nature produces hers; but as, in fact, many important qualities of oil-painting cannot be obtained in a hurry, the attempt to copy Nature at her own speed usually leads to false or incomplete relations of tone and colour. The ideally best practice, if the memory were strong enough for it, would be that of Nazon, who gazed intently at nature so long as the effect lasted, and then went home to paint it.

I need not dwell upon impressionism any longer at the present time, as it is important only because all the other sectarian doctrines have ceased to be militant in France. Nobody thinks in these days of entering into controversy on the exhausted subjects of classicism, romanticism, or realism. In literature the case is not exactly the same, since under the name of realism a certain class of French novelists have found a pretext for pandering to the lowest instincts of human nature. The popular support for 'realism' in literature which has been obtained by this device has given it a prolonged importance; but in painting realism is dead as a separate doctrine, though it influences much art that does not bear its name. No country has been more divided into bitterly hostile sects than France — yet there, as elsewhere, time has proved that in the fine arts these divisions are not lasting, and a dispassionate criticism may show that they were never complete or profound. The well-known rustic painter, Jules Breton, showed lately in his autobiography that some of the most heretical painters of his time had continued a tradition of art from the old masters, so that their works, when hung in the Louvre, were neither discordant nor out of place there. The art of Millet, supposed to be rustic realism, is no doubt rustic and contains a good deal of reality, but beneath its apparent simplicity lies the unobtrusive study of the old artistic problems of line, light, mass, and composition. Any bigoted sectarianism in art is vain; for art, when it *is* art, is all one in reality. A new doctrine and practice may arise, and seem at first peculiar because excessive; then efforts are made to improve away defects, and with the defects go the peculiarities, and so we get back to something much resembling the old art again. There was plenty of realism before Courbet, and of classicism before the *néo - Grecs*. Artists had painted in broad, out-of-doors daylight before the modern French invented the *plein air*. Still, there are changes of fashion, and there have certainly been some extensions of the domain of art; the old narrowness and intolerance have ceased to act as a restraint. A landscape painter may paint the greens of nature which were forbidden to him in the first quarter of this century, and a figure painter is at liberty to represent any costume that takes his fancy, if only it is authentic with regard to the epoch he has chosen. The only crime forbidden to a French artist in the present day is the *vieux jeu*. His style of painting must not be old-fashioned. It may be outrageous, it may sin against all artistic decorum, but it must never be behind the age. A member of the French school died lately after having survived his reputation. He went on painting as before with at least equal knowledge and increased experience, but his works became unsaleable. I asked a Parisian dealer if he could explain the case to me. 'Facilement,' he replied; 'son style est démodé, c'est vieux jeu.' His style had gone out; and yet there are other styles contemporary with his, for example, those of Corot and Millet, which have not gone out. The case would be more explicable if all artists fashionable at one time became unfashionable, ten years later, together, but that is not what happens. One man's style is condemned as *vieux jeu*, whilst another, equally *vieux jeu* in reality, is never called so. The true explanation is that a style is condemned as old-fashioned when it comes to be out of favour; if it maintains or increases its popularity we hear nothing about its being old-fashioned. In the case of the French artist alluded to, the damnatory *vieux jeu* means simply 'not in demand at present.'

From an independent and philosophical point of view these changes of fashion are a subject of curiosity interesting as a revelation of the degree of knowledge or seriousness that there may be in the popular appreciation of art. The value of the *Angelus* of Millet was, when painted, *nothing*. His friend, Arthur Stevens, could not find a purchaser either for the *Woodcutter* or the *Angelus*. Meanwhile the artist and his family were literally starving; they had no wood for fire, they had no credit; how they managed to get a little food is a mystery. Millet was ill with anxiety, his wife was going to be confined, and he said, 'It is impossible to get what we need.' He was suffering from 'painter's poverty' in its worst form. Not a Frenchman would look at the *Angelus*. At last it was purchased by a Belgian for seventy-two pounds. It was sold in 1890 to a French tradesman for thirty thousand pounds. Now, this is what a change of fashion means. With fashion against him an artist is a miserable pauper, with fashion in his favour he may buy mansions and estates, his own merit being precisely the same in both cases. Had the quality of Millet's picture improved between 1859 and 1890? No, it had deteriorated; but at the first date the French did not care for Millet, and at the second they had elevated him to the rank of a *gloire nationale*. Just now, fifteen years after his death, Millet, so far from being *démodé*, has become *la mode* itself. A case of an opposite character, though not so excessive in the difference, is that of Toulmouche, who died last year. Toulmouche was at one time quite in the first rank of society painters; he was the painter of little insignificant incidents that may happen in elegant interiors; incidents which, in art, are merely an excuse for pretty arrangements of figures and furniture, with suitable backgrounds of panelled walls, looking-glasses, marble chimney-pieces with the ornaments on them, and so on. The public that left Millet to starve kept Toulmouche in great comfort until the day when he ceased to be fashionable, and then it deserted him. He bore the change like a philosopher, knowing that he had done good work of its kind, and that the reputation he formerly enjoyed had not been undeserved.

Just now the qualities most in favour in France are freshness and straightforwardness of workmanship, showing the work, and I should say that of all mental qualities sharpness of perception and sincerity go for most in the present day, whilst industry and polish, the laboured correction of slow intellects, count for much less than in the earlier part of the century.   These tendencies have been connected with the increased favour shown to three other arts—etching, water-colour, and pastel.   So far as French etching has been original, and not the interpretation of pictures, it has shown a tendency to free and sincere sketching rather than to finish.   French water-colour is usually very direct in handling, showing the work plainly, and French pastel is as frank as it is rapid—so frank, indeed, that in some of the best-known examples beauty is less sought after than truth of character.   The taste which is dominant just now may be made intelligible by saying that if Franz Hals were in existence he would stand in the first rank of contemporary artists, whereas if he had appeared in France in the generation preceding ours he would probably have failed to earn a living.

The increased practice of out-of-door study has done much to make conventional art unpopular.   For example, there is the well-known picture of the *Martyrdom* (or the moment before martyrdom) *of St Symphorien*, by Ingres, one of his most important and representative works.   In the background there is the Roman gateway of Autun and a patch of sky.   The lighting is so arbitrary that nobody can tell what time of day it is, and the tones of the distant gateway are so false that its masonry could not assume them under any circumstances. Modern study of open daylight makes painting of this kind look as if it belonged to the Dark Ages.   Without being professed landscape painters, contemporary French artists do now, in almost all cases, accept so far the teaching of external nature that they are not afraid of plain daylight, with the various greys of true shadows, sometimes almost blue by contrast, quite unlike the umbers that used to be the favourite shadow colours.   Others go further, and attempt the study of full southern sunshine, with its glare when it falls on all light objects, its cool shadows, its powerful reflections, and its open skies, dark by contrast, and often almost leaden-hued with heat.

A very common characteristic of modern French painting is the dislike to artificial arrangements in composition, or to anything that looks like them.   A carefully composed picture, in the present day, runs some risk of being condemned as *vieux jeu* unless the artifices of its arrangement have been very carefully concealed, and it is not easy to conceal them from the keen eye of professional artists.   This subject of composition reminds me of a story told about a French artist who was setting out on a sketching tour.   One of his brethren strongly dissuaded him from going where he intended.   'You must not sketch there,' he said, 'because the material is so good, so pictorial, and it comes together so well that people will accuse you of having composed;' a fate that actually befell the present writer on account of some sketches on the Saône which were said to be 'theatrical'—like the natural moon that the young lady declared to be 'so like the moon in "Norma."'   There are, however, a considerable number of recent French pictures that would never, I should imagine, incur the imputation of having been composed, even from their worst enemies.   In others there is some care about arrangement without any study of composition.   In some, composition is laborious but studiously concealed.   However this may be, it is certain that the old art of elaborate and toilsome composition, displaying itself obviously throughout the whole scheme of a picture, is now very little in favour, and I have met with instances of arrangements intentionally *contrariés* that they might not look too orderly.   Besides this, the new school has (speaking generally) a strong tendency to the selection of commonplace subjects, relying for success on the skill with which the simple materials are represented.   A painter is struck by the devotional attitude of some old woman in a church, so he paints her just as she is, with the plain bench she is sitting upon and the whitewashed wall behind her, not seeking for any adventitious interest or ornament.   One great advantage of this taste for simple subjects is their unity.   Certainly, French painters of the present day very frequently, and, I must say, very generally, keep this virtue of unity in their works.   For example, the picture of M. Dawant which accompanies this paper has the quality in a very

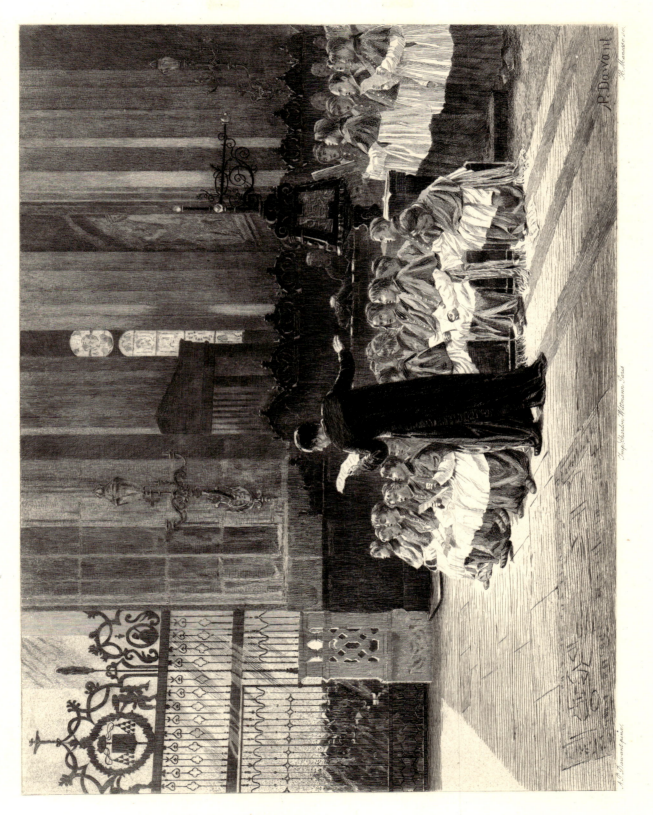

A. Davant

Imp. Chardon Wittmann, Paris

A. Davant pinx.

THE CHORISTERS

high degree. It is called *Une Maîtrise d'Enfants, Souvenir d'Italie.* The word *maîtrise*, in this sense, means a school for choristers.* The pupils have met for a rehearsal, not in their school, but in the cathedral itself, and they are in full costume, as for an impending function. Their scarlet and white give them a very brilliant appearance, and in this picture are relieved most effectually by the dark oak of the stalls, the greys of the columns and pavements, and the valuable intense black of the cassock worn by the chapel-master himself. The details of the interior are painted with great care and perfect truth, but they do not distract our attention from the master and his boys, all very characteristic of a *maîtrise* and all absorbed by one occupation. This picture may be taken as representative of a large class of works in the French school in its quietly truthful representation of observed reality. And if there is not much obvious composition, there is considerable judgment in the use of the materials, in the massing of them to the right and in the greater openness and space and light towards the left. The reader has only to imagine a dark wall or heavy close pillars in place of the grating with the cardinal's arms to perceive the value of that grating in its place : the light marble with its open work catching the sunshine and the gleam of sunshine on the pavement complete the luminous arrangement of that end of the picture as opposed to the gloom of the other.

There is one department of art which allows modern artists to combine their love of exact truth with the picturesque, both in colour and composition. Military painters have at their disposal an endless supply of material that is at the same time varied and what artists call 'amusing,' and when they are tired of present military fashions they can easily recur to the past, with plenty of documentary evidence to help them. It is true that battle pictures have often, like hunting scenes, been rather a discouragement to the critic, who, for some reason, too frequently fails to derive from them the peculiar and exquisite pleasure that we now call 'aesthetic.' What acres of 'battle-pieces' have been painted, and by clever men too, that nobody would wish to add to any well-selected national gallery ; one would give most of them, rather, to the mess-rooms of regiments or the class-rooms of military schools. The reason seems to be that military painting passes so easily into a sort of manufacture, the materials of it are so glaring, glittering, and abundant, and so easily made to cover great spaces of canvas. Several modern French artists have done much to redeem military painting from the sort of discredit into which it had fallen after Horace Vernet, who, though himself a man with extraordinary gifts, was still something of the canvas-coverer in his day. The remarkable industry and seriousness of purpose that belong to the nature of Meissonier have enabled him to show that as much industry and learning could be expended on this branch of art as on any other, whilst the brilliant abilities of De Neuville and Detaille have been exercised along with the humbler quality of accuracy, the result of painstaking observation. Since De Neuville died, his rival is almost alone in the special profession of military painting. He is unquestionably a most vigorous and brilliant artist, answering quite accurately in art to the best qualities of the best French officers, their liveliness, quickness of apprehension, grasp of detail, and decision. His last picture, *Vive l'Empereur !* a charge of the Fourth Hussars in 1807, is an effective example of the artist's work in the full strength of his maturity, and though it has just been observed that military pictures are not always what one cares to see added to national galleries, it is not surprising that a generous and patriotic Frenchman, who desires to remain unknown, should have purchased this work for the Luxembourg. The canvas is of large size, and is chiefly occupied by the leading officer, who, with his sword uplifted and the scabbard flying behind him, dashes forward in the

---

* The word originally means simply 'mastery.' In a secondary sense it means the employment of an ecclesiastical music-master, and, again, the house in which he lives, or, by extension, the assemblage of scholars under his guidance, whether they meet in his house or elsewhere. In the picture before us they have met in the choir of some cathedral church ; but there may be a *maîtrise* where there is no cathedral. A general as well as a musical education is given.

first heat of onset. His grey charger, as yet unscathed, is in a condition of intense excitement, and though not shrinking from his duty seems to know how terrible before him is the glittering hedge of bayonets. Of all actions in military life there is not one, unless it be the storming of a citadel, in which excitement is so concentrated as in a charge of cavalry. It is the supreme moment of a cavalry-soldier's life, and in M. Detaille's picture we have the full stir and energy of it, the trumpeters sounding the charge horses starting suddenly at full gallop, sword-blades flashing ready for their deadly work, uniforms as yet brilliant and unsoiled by dust and blood. The picture is full of bright and light colour, which of course has come much darker in the photogravure, red uniforms, rich ornaments, and the little there is of landscape in tones of pale red and green. The year 1807 may seem far from us now, but unhappily the interest of these war pictures is not really in the past, it is in the light they throw on the still more terrible contests of the future. Europe has not seen the last cavalry-charge ; not for the last time has the artilleryman been jolted on a gun-carriage as the team galloped over the rough ground of a battle-field.

II

Painting ; the Observation of Contemporary Life

THE art of the painter has this in common with the art of the novelist, that whatever may be its excursions in the regions of history or poetry, its first exercises must always be in the representation of the life which the student can see with his own eyes. Even when a painter like Paul Baudry decorates a great opera-house with allegorical figures, all the knowledge that he is able to put into his designs, and without which they would be empty and valueless, is derived from the patient study of the living model ; and when a novelist like Flaubert attempts the revival of the past in a laborious work of reconstruction like 'Salammbô,' whatever vitality such a creation may possess is really derived from the observation which is more visible to the ordinary reader in a study of his own times like 'Madame Bovary.' The whole truth about the relation of Art to Nature may be expressed in a very few words. Art derives all its suggestions and all its science from Nature, but it makes use of them with a certain liberty that is indispensable to the exercise of either taste or invention. There is no hope for a school that is blind to the interest of the common world ; there can only be a vague and distant prospect of true success for a school that binds itself down to the literal copyism of nature ; but there is every chance of success for a school that keeps up at the same time a lively interest in the life around it and the love of culture, that is, an intelligent deference for the artistic experience of the past. Now, although we cannot speak justly in the same terms of all contemporary French artists, some of whom are much more observant of contemporary life than others, the truth still remains that many active and well-known members of the younger French school seem to be always looking about them for what is interesting in work and in leisure, in dress, incident, and behaviour. There might have been a tendency to notice only those varieties of human labour already illustrated and recognised by great artists. For example, ploughing with oxen is ancient, Virgilian, and poetical. The ruder the implement and the harness, the more primitive the costume of the peasant, the more poetical the subject becomes. Would any artist venture on such a subject as steam-ploughing ? A modern Frenchman would be likely to attempt it if he could see his way to make the subject artistically interesting. I remember a picture of a mowing machine, not without some freshness of interest in the seat or perch of the driver, really much safer than it looks ; and I have a recollection, too, of a modern threshing machine in a picture, interesting by the atmospheric effects of its smoke and steam and its clouds of dust, as well as humanly interesting from the sustained and feverish activity of the vigorous rustics who served it. The slow advance of the irresistible steam-roller on a public road, with its herald marching in advance to announce its coming, and the frightened horses that it meets, is also possible as a subject, being very expressive as an example of weight and force ; whilst of all human contrivances that which best conveys the idea of speed is evidently an express train. In the Salon of 1887 there was a picture by M. Ferré representing the rapid passage of such a train through a quiet potato-field, the peasant-women pausing in their work to look at it. Here is a much stronger contrast than any that was within the reach of painters in the eighteenth century. The slow monotony of peasant-life is suddenly intruded upon for half a minute by the rush of the locomotive.

D

Here, the quiet, almost mindless labour ; there, the triumphant result of science and skill, strong as a thousand horses, swift as an eagle on the wing. Here, in the field, the plodding, ancient ways ; there, in the train, the arts, the wealth, the luxury of Paris, whirled past to some distant capital. It will be found, I imagine, in most things, that whilst old methods of work are more picturesque than those of the modern time, they are often less impressive. An armourer of the fifteenth century making a helmet or a breastplate is undoubtedly an excellent subject for painting, but though we may admire his skill, his work does not convey so striking an idea of human power as the forging of armour for an iron-clad. The tools used in modern metallurgy are so tremendous, and the disciplined unity of action amongst the workmen has to be so perfect, that the mind is overawed by them, and, so far, they are highly favourable to art. The only remaining question is whether the effects of light and the qualities of colour in scenes of this kind are such as an artist cares for. Certainly I have witnessed effects, both at Sheffield and at the Creusot, that would have delighted Rembrandt and exercised his utmost power. The chiaroscuro abounds in powerful oppositions, and the colour, in sombre hues, is full of richness and depth, bursting into sudden occasional splendour in the glow of the furnace light. A scene of this kind was truthfully and energetically painted by M. Rixens in his *Laminage de l'Acier* (steel - rolling), in the Salon of 1887. For the quality of unity no better subject could be found, because the men are all working together, in eager excitement, for one and the same purpose, and animated by a common thought. There is less excitement and not quite so much unity of action, though equal unity of idea, in M. E. Chaperon's picture of a military bakery, *Le Pain de Munition*, in the Salon of 1888.

THE EXPRESS. BY M. FERRÉ.

Another work by the same artist, *La Douche au Régiment* (1887), showed how French soldiers follow the healthy practice of washing each other with a powerful jet of water from a hose, as if they were extinguishing a fire. These pictures are entirely modern, and show truthfully the more prosaic aspects of military life ; and here I may notice a tendency in the modern school to illustrate military life as it is in those details which require ordinary patience, and afford no opportunity for display. This is only one more proof of that remarkable sobering of the French mind which has resulted partly from the war of 1870 and partly from increased political experience.

The antagonism that used to exist between science and the fine arts appears to have given place to a certain degree of sympathy. For several years past there has been evidence in the Salon of an increasing interest in the work of surgeons, chemists, anatomists, and students of natural history. It seems almost as if Art were turning her back on her own domain of beauty, to look consciously over the wall that separates it from her sister's domain of knowledge. This curiosity seems to have answered to a corresponding curiosity in the public mind, as many of these pictures of scientific work have excited much interest and have been widely disseminated in black and white. They seem all to have one characteristic in common, which I take to be due to the contagion of the scientific spirit—a remarkable exactness of representation. A picture by M. Brouillet attracted great attention in the Salon

of 1887. It was entitled, *A Clinical Lesson at the Salpêtrière*, and represented a woman in a
fit, with Dr. Charcot lecturing to his pupils on the nature and symptoms of the attack. Nothing

STEEL-ROLLING. BY M. RIXENS.

was more curious in that work than the extreme and equal care bestowed upon the most commonplace details of costume and building, in themselves not worth an artist's attention for a

LE PAIN DE MUNITION. BY M. E. CHAPERON.

moment, yet deriving an adventitious importance from the spectator's interest in the dreadful
place and in the terrible maladies that are treated there. Many other pictures of the same
class have appealed during the last few years to the public desire for veracity. I happened to
visit a lunatic asylum a few days before writing this page, and the pitiable inmates in the garden

—tree, yet carefully watched—reminded me strongly of the famous picture by J. Béraud, *Les Fous*, in the Salon of 1885. That picture represented the grounds of an asylum, with fifteen or twenty lunatics busying themselves aimlessly, or stopping suddenly, as they will, in profound if profitless meditation. The foreground figure was especially striking—a man in a frock-coat, the pockets of it stuffed with papers of vast importance to him ; his arms folded ; his gaze wandering over the enclosure with an air of conscious superiority. There was little aesthetic pleasure or charm, but an unflinching truthfulness, even in the careful painting of the thin tree-stems, the low walls, and the sanded walk. It is the same with all these modern French pictures of pathological or even only scientific subjects—they are invariably quiet, painstaking, unpretending, and the artists appear to accept even the most unpromising material that can be found in the plainest buildings. M. Dagnan-Bouveret painted

AFTER THE OPERATION. BY M. BISSON.

a *Vaccination* — women bringing children to be vaccinated in some country *mairie*. Nothing in this work seemed to be embellished— the story was told so simply, and the painter had not sought for the rural picturesque — yet the picture produced its effect, and was followed by others, such as M. Scalbert's *Vaccination gratuite à Paris*, in the Salon of 1890, painted exactly on the same principles. Three or four years previously M. Gueldry chose to paint the interior of the municipal laboratory in Paris, which is much less elegant than an ordinary chemist's shop, but, I believe, he omitted nothing. M. Laurent Gsell exhibited in 1890 *Une Leçon de Manipulation chimique à la Faculté de Médecine*, the lesson being given in a remarkably unpicturesque interior. There have been many other pictures of this class, all descended from the *Anatomical Lessons*, which began to be painted when artists took an interest in dissection ; but there is this difference, that whilst a painter like Rembrandt thought about art in the treatment of such a subject, these modern Frenchmen appear to think only of veracity. The picture by M. Bisson, *After the Operation*, exhibited last year, is, however, composed with a degree of care that reminds us of old-fashioned ideas. The group is extremely natural, yet any one who is accustomed to artistic arrangements will find them, not only in the figures, but in all the accessories as well.

The secret of the interest of these pictures, which are popular enough to be regularly reproduced in the illustrated newspapers, is that people like to see the doings of scientific men, who usually work in privacy, and they have a curiosity about such places as lunatic asylums which the picture satisfies without requiring them to visit the unpleasant places themselves. The public have faith, too, in the veracity and observation of the artist when he represents what he has seen and studied on the spot, so that these works command a degree of credence which is never quite accorded to pictures representing another age. This desire for veracity in the public, and readiness to satisfy it in the artist, are, however, more favourable to honesty in study than to the exercise of invention and imagination, or even to manual power in the technical art of painting. Works of this class are usually observant but without invention, and although their execution is painstaking in the extreme, as all execution must be when simple truth is the object, whilst there is no shirking of tasks that are at the same time difficult and artistically unrewarding, still this careful conscientious work is not in itself delightful. There is, at least for me, more ocular pleasure in the tender and graceful execution of some little landscape sketched in oil from nature by Isenbart, a painter not yet famous, but gifted with an exquisite sense of landscape beauty, than in many of those scientific figure-pictures whose photographic veracity appears to satisfy the public. I fully believe, however, that this very truthful art will leave works of enduring interest as a representation of our time, and that future generations will find in them the same value, as records, that Dutch works of the seventeenth century have for us. The essential difference is, that whilst Dutch art was not always beautiful it was, at least, almost invariably picturesque and made pleasant to the eye by the charms of light-and-shade, colour, and execution. The picture by M. Victor Marec in the Salon of 1888, '*Ici on est mieux qu'en face*,' is a good subject for comparison with Dutch art. It is like a page out of a realistic French novel. A party of working people have been to a funeral; they have just left the cemetery and have stopped to refresh themselves in a *cabaret* opposite the gates. They are in their Sunday clothes, and yet their class is as accurately marked as it could be if Daudet reported their conversation. The human interest is deeper, too, than it would have been in an old Dutch picture. There is much pathos in the solitary grief of the elderly woman in the foreground, who sits silently thinking of the dead whilst her neighbour in a big shawl has fixed her eye upon her, not very delicately perhaps, yet seriously and not without sympathy. The others talk with various degrees of animation, except a bearded man in a soft hat who leans his chin upon his hand and meditates. The interior, the costumes, the furniture, are all absolutely unpicturesque. The square windows, the plain tables, the common rush-bottomed chairs, do not, altogether, offer as much artistic interest as a sawn barrel painted by Teniers, nor are all these vulgar wine-bottles worth a Dutchman's jug of ale. The interest here is human and dramatic rather than pictorial, and when I see a picture of this kind hung on the walls of an exhibition and the people interested in it, as they naturally are, by the life in it and the contrast with death in the cemetery, I cannot help thinking of the disastrous effect of such a picture in any gallery already rich in works artistically of a higher kind. Yet the work is perfectly blameless from a moral point of view, and there is more intellect in it than in many a thing of beauty which its owner cherishes as a joy for ever. It is a result less of art than of photographic and literary influences.

In the Salon of 1887 there was a picture of ordinary life by M. Fourié, entitled *A Wedding Feast at Yport*, representing one of those provincial wedding breakfasts that last interminably in the lower middle classes. This time the feast is spread in the open air amongst the trees of a garden, and one of the men sits at ease in his shirt-sleeves, whilst another in the same costume is clinking glasses with a lady. The picture was quite true to the kind of life it represented, and was a very effective specimen of what has been called 'democratic art.' The best art of this kind shows the people fairly as they are, without either exaggerating vulgarity by caricature, or lending to ordinary folks an ideal refinement and distinction that they do not in reality possess. M. Fourié's picture was one of the successes of its year amongst the 'democratic' works, and it had some definite artistic qualities, for although the forms of the people were necessarily and representatively commonplace, the scene gained a certain brilliance by the skilful opposition of lights and darks, and the place represented was not without some pleasantness and beauty. The artist,

E

too, had worked in a right temper, not being contemptuous in his treatment of the uncultivated class.

This kind of painting, satisfied with the representation of everyday life exactly as it is and without ideal aspiration, has the same right to exist that we all accord to simple and truthful prose, but if it were to become predominant in a school there would be little hope of artistic pre-eminence. There is in the French school an intermediate class of work that takes its place between commonplace realism and the artistic ideal. M. Geoffroy appears to be one of the best and artistically most successful of those painters who observe nature closely without forgetting the culture or losing sight of the aspirations of an artist. His sympathy with children is a great help to the human interest of his pictures. In the Universal Exhibition of 1889 there was a delightful picture by him showing us eighteen

A WEDDING FEAST AT YPORT. BY M. FOURIÉ.

or twenty little boys diligently at work during their writing lesson. There they were, busy as in life, and in the manner peculiar to children, with their own ways of holding of head and the pen, or in the case of the smaller boys the slate-pencil. The artist had reserved for himself certain rights of arrangement in costume and attitude so as to obtain effective contrasts, to break the monotony of a line, and to gain variety of individual manners in the monotony of an identical occupation. Another very charming work by the same artist was *The Lavatory at the Maternal School*, exhibited at the Salon of 1885. The washing-basins are fixed in a low table in the middle of the room, and the children are already washing or waiting for their turn, watched over by two mistresses. The picture was prettily conceived and as well and carefully composed, though without any ostentation of art, as if it had been an illustration of some classical or biblical subject. Even in the pathetic picture of *Visiting Day at the Hospital* (1889), though the materials are simple in the extreme, and even unpromising, they are arranged with an artist's taste. Observe the use of the *table de nuit* on the left and also of the curtains to frame the pretty distance where a sister is kissing her little brother. I need not expatiate on the quiet weariness of the nearer invalid, calm but languid and not equal to much talking or animation. M. Geoffroy's sympathy with the young is powerfully shown in the picture

Ben Damman.   Geoffroy. pxt.

CHILL PENURY.

in the Luxembourg, *Les Infortunés*, of which a careful etching by M. Damman accompanies this chapter. The poor children here have been bred in the worst of sanitary conditions, they have been badly lodged in foul air with insufficient food, and they are in a very low physical state, marked most observedly and minutely by the artist. Still, in order that our sympathy might not be interfered with by repulsion, he has avoided the degenerate type of character. These poor children are not destined to be rascals or curses of society, but only sufferers, and perhaps a burden upon a world that has neglected to look to them in time. The delicate artistic sense of M. Geoffroy is shown as plainly in this picture as in the others that I have mentioned. If the subject is painful the presentation of it is attractive, and there is a quality in the painting itself that cannot be fully interpreted in another art.

Of all modern French painters it is certainly M. Pelez whose sympathy with the suffering classes expresses itself with the most poignant force. His picture, *Un Nid de Misère* (1887), seemed to me one of the most profoundly touching representations of poverty that I had ever seen. There is no single English word that translates *misère* exactly. It means the final state of utter wretchedness that is brought on by total destitution. A pen sketch gives some idea of the subject and motive, but the picture itself was as painfully affecting as a sight of the reality. It was appropriately sad in colour, and did not attempt to offer any pleasure to the eye, but there the poor children were, sleeping and forgetting for an

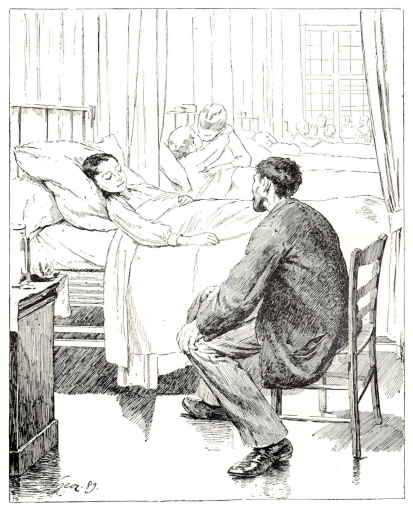

VISITING DAY AT THE HOSPITAL. BY M. GEOFFROY.

hour the already grievous burden of existence. It is a burden that the strong, the clever, the resolute may bear with a triumphant sense of difficulty overcome, but it is a crushing weight on feeble shoulders like those of these poor weaklings. I believe there is no contemporary artist whose human sympathies are so profound or so constant as those of M. Pelez. Some of his pictures are liable, at first sight, to be misunderstood—their humane sentiment is not always obvious to the careless glance of a visitor to exhibitions, nor is it always explained by the title in the catalogue, but it is generally, if not invariably, the determining motive of the work.

'Democratic' art need not be confined to the poorer classes, for democracy is not the equivalent of poverty. The French democracy includes a well-to-do middle class, and also a rich mercantile and upper professional class that lives very comfortably and expensively without being aristocratic either in principles or aspirations. The ambition to belong to the aristocracy when one is not born in it is chiefly found amongst minor rural landowners; the rich middle class is usually urban.   M. Béraud seems to know that class as well as the easily accessible frequenters of the *brasseries*, or the bawling demagogues in the political clubs.   He paints the crowded drawing - rooms of rich townspeople with the keenest observation and an incisive truth, not without a touch of satire, especially in his quiet refusal to help tailors and dressmakers to any further improvement of the human form.   After looking at a few pictures by such artists as Béraud, Fourié, Chaperon, and Marec, a foreigner might know

UN NID DE MISÈRE. BY M. PELEZ.

the external aspects and manners of the French democracy as if he had lived amongst it. One cannot affirm that it is a poetical democracy ; it is, in reality, very matter-of-fact and prosaic, and it is not free from considerable faults and vices, but it has some virtues, too, the chief of which is industry, usually accompanied by a courageous and cheerful temper. It deserved, no doubt, to be celebrated in art, the only misfortune being that the more truthful these democratic pictures become, the less they satisfy the desires of the aesthetic sense.

III

Various Effects of Modern Observation

A WELL-KNOWN French critic, M. Albert Wolff, admitted in the year 1888 that 'the French school lives in observation rather than in imagination,' that 'the reality of things is the mark of contemporary art,' and that 'the exceptional works of each Salon belong to this order of ideas;' in a word, to the idea of naturalism, if it can be truly said that naturalism is an idea. Then M. Wolff went on to say that the pictures most interesting to the modern French public were those which represented life exactly, and not so much the life of the past, however accurate the revival, as that of the present day. Instead of enhancing the interest of a subject by illustrating it with a reference to antiquity, the modern Frenchman usually finds by experience that it pays better, in the attention drawn to his work and the money it brings, to represent old subjects in the most modern forms. In the Salon of 1890 there was a picture by M. Brouillet which attracted universal attention. It was entitled *Suzanne* without any further explanation, but the name at once recalls Susannah and the Elders to the French mind. The modern Susannah is a young woman of the *demi-monde*, sitting in a *café*, and simultaneously receiving the addresses of two well-clad elderly Frenchmen. The subject is externally much more decent than in the well-known picture by Rubens, but it had been almost used up in the old form, and gained, no doubt, a certain freshness and piquancy by being represented as a 'page' of contemporary Parisian life. The work was so full of reality that to see it was to be transported at once into a *café* and become, as no doubt the painter himself had been, an observer of the actual incident.

The interest of this 'modern instance' was rather that of life than art, for it needs very little reflection to perceive that the biblical narrative, as interpreted by the old masters, was far superior, artistically, to this Parisian translation. The nudity of the original Susannah is finer for painting than the fashions of 1890, and the Oriental costumes of the original Elders were far more available material than the silk hats and correct tailoring of two rich elderly Parisians. This comparison brings us precisely to the centre of the whole subject. The interest of this modern French art is not, in most cases, so much artistic as human. I mean to say that when the modern French artist of the new school (there are exceptions, but I am speaking generally just now) has to make his choice between an artistic advantage on the one hand and some additional piquancy of human interest on the other, he will generally go where his public lead him. The consequence is that in a very great number of modern pictures art is sacrificed to mere fact. I happen to be writing this chapter in Paris, and just before coming to these lines I passed an important picture-shop on the Boulevards which afforded some interesting examples of downright modernism, and amongst others this. The picture represented one of those charming river landscapes that abound in France. On one side was a noble mass of trees, on the other a slope of land, and beyond them a hilly but not mountainous distance. Between the spectator and that distance stood a factory with its long chimney, duly emitting smoke. The artist, no doubt, was of opinion (and he was right) that the factory added the interest of life and industry to his subject; he did not think of, or he did not care about, the artistic injury that the hideous building inflicted upon a beautiful landscape, and he appears to have been entirely destitute of that fine sense which establishes a clear distinction between the poetic and the prosaic industries of men. This negligence or insensibility seems to be increasingly frequent in the new school. Many of the painters either do not know what a very delicate, easily destroyed charm is the charm of art, or else they consider themselves strong enough to do without it by appealing to the public interest in fidelity of representation and in the facts of everyday life. Certainly the power of imitating things very closely is a misfortune for painting, not as a manual trade, nor as a subject of popular curiosity, but as a fine art. In music the art is much purer, and as a rule more elevated, by being restricted to the artistic sphere, and in consequence of the feebleness of its imitative powers.

The inconvenience of imitative art from the imaginative point of view is most visible in those works that attempt to combine fact with imagination. The best instance of this was a picture by Gérôme, in the Salon of 1888 : it was entitled *The Poet touched by the Muse*, and it represented a gentleman in the costume of Lamartine's youth, reclining at ease on the sea-shore. He was painted with praiseworthy accuracy and truth down to his short whiskers, his cravat, the high collar of his cloak, his buttons, and his boots—the boots, in particular, being a perfect fit, and evidently as good as new. The poet had laid down his hat and gloves with his cane, and was contemplating the sea, when the Muse, bearing her lyre, put her forefinger on his curly occiput. This is the reason why the sea-shore was crowded with female beauty—Venus standing on the crest of a wave and a score of lovely attendants disporting themselves where land and water meet. Neptune, too, is coming shorewards with his white horses, and all for the entertainment of the gentleman in boots, rude nature being represented by a flock of seals on his right hand, but to these he pays no attention. A picture of this kind is really little less than a disaster, because it mixes the most incongruous elements, modern tailoring with antique mythology, and also because it gives fiction without making it credible and acceptable by any ideality of conception or of treatment.

A more fortunate instance of the mixture of reality with fancy was the well-known picture of *The Dream*, by Detaille, exhibited in the Salon of 1888, and afterwards purchased for the Luxembourg. A regiment of soldiers are lying in their cloaks during a bivouac, their muskets stacked in a long line far over the undulating plain. In the sky are phantom warriors of an earlier time, apparently of the First Empire—their flags waving, their cocked hats carried high on their bayonets in a moment of eager enthusiasm. The dream may be of former victories, of some Marengo or Austerlitz, in the midst of the weary discouragements of 1870. It is not the first time that phantoms or dream-visions have been represented in the sky. Turner did it with a rare success in the little vignette representing the Vision of Columbus, but in Turner's vignette, reality occupied a very small space. In the picture by Detaille, it is conspicuous and very carefully studied, even down to such a small matter as the case containing an officer's field-glass, and the minute details, all accurate, of swords, rifles, and trumpets. Still, since in this picture the vision itself is that of a past reality, the contrast is not nearly so shocking as in M. Gérôme's work, where a poet in modern boots is touched by the Muse carrying a lyre. Besides this, the sleeping soldiers are hidden in the drapery of their cloaks. The picture is exceedingly impressive, but it might have been equally so as a simple bivouac, without the dream-phantoms in the sky.

It is always dangerous to translate a purely literary expression into the definite forms of precise art. In the Salon of 1888 there was a picture by M. Realier-Dumas, illustrating the expression of Napoleon I.—'I found the crown of France on the floor, and I picked it up.' The scene represented is in one of the saloons of the Tuileries at the time of its pillage by the mob. The royal mantle lies spread like a torn and disordered carpet in the middle of the polished oak *parquet*, and on the mantle is the crown, as if it had rolled on the floor and been stopped by the thick folds of the ermine. Napoleon, his arms crossed and in the pose of a statue, looks at the glittering object out of the corner of his eye. Everything in the picture is represented with the closest accuracy, down to the clever joiner's work of the *parquet*; but we feel at once that it is a laborious, literal, and prosaic materialisation of a striking figure of speech. This, I think, is the misfortune of the present French literal school—it is observant of what can be seen and measured, such as locksmiths' work, joinery, tailoring, and shoemaking; but it is too unimaginative to deal with ideas that are not precisely within the range of the measurable and the tangible.

One feels this even with regard to subjects in themselves of no great imaginative interest, and which, it might be thought, require little beyond close observation in the artist. Perhaps the reader may remember Rosa Bonheur's *Horse Fair*. If he does not know the first large picture he probably knows the smaller replica in the National Gallery, or at least the engraving, and even that is enough for the purposes of my argument. Rosa Bonheur is not a great artist as the imaginative artists are great, but she has excellent judgment; she knows perfectly well what may be introduced into a picture with advantage and what it is wiser to avoid. In the background of her *Horse Fair* she gave enough of local truth to fix the place, but she gave it lightly, without insisting

COFFEE-GRINDING. BY L. POMEY.

upon it, and she intentionally obscured the background with the dust raised by the trotting horses. Two or three years ago M. Grandjean painted the same subject—and now observe the effect of recent realism, of the present matter-of-fact spirit, on his picture. Near the place where his trotting horses turn there is a common gas-lamp with three lights, and it is painted with photographic accuracy. In the distance are rows of Parisian houses, without the slightest interest of any artistic or architectural kind, yet M. Grandjean did not omit them or sketch them slightly; he took pains to copy them as they were in reality. One does not condemn such industry, particularly as in this case the horses were painted with the utmost truth; still, the difference between Rosa Bonheur and M. Grandjean marks the peculiar sort of progress that has been made by the French School since the foundation of the Republic, a progress in the direction of accuracy and away from the old (now old-fashioned) caution and care in the selection and in the treatment of materials.

In the last chapter I happened to mention a picture of steel-rolling by M. Rixens, but was not aware that it had been purchased by the Municipality for the Hôtel de Ville. On going through that building I found the picture hanging in a council chamber, in a place of honour, with a picture also illustrating labour on each side of it. These works had been purchased for social or democratic reasons, and two important pictures of street move-ments in the Revolutions of 1793 and 1848 had been bought for political reasons; there were action and energy in all of them, but remarkably little beauty. Then the reflection occurred to me that the architecture of the new Hôtel de Ville manifests the most scru-pulous care for beauty throughout, even down to such details as the panelling of passages and the locksmith's work on the doors, yet that the ugly and the common, after being expelled from architecture, came back in the shape of painting, and were hung up in great gilt frames with as much honour as could have been given in Venice to the ideals of Titian or Tintoret. The same reflection occurred to me again before some new mural paintings at the Sorbonne, to which we shall come in due time. It is a strange and curious result of the modern matter-of-fact spirit that whilst architecture is strict in its rejection of the incongruous, or at least endeavours to be so, being *elegant* in the original sense of the word, which implies a careful choice, the sister art of painting shows less and less of a right and necessary fastidiousness as time goes on. The difference appears to be that whilst architecture (as distinct from mere building) is a pure fine art, like music, painting is more comparable to writing, which may be sometimes a fine art and sometimes a mere record of facts, without any charm of selection, *ordonnance*, or idealisation.

Much of contemporary French art, like modern art elsewhere, is remarkable for poverty of invention. The subjects selected are often of the very slightest interest in themselves, and not enhanced by the charm that is always conferred, even on the barest materials, by the power of the inventive imagination when it is present. However, this gift is so rare, especially in prosaic times like these, that it would be too much to expect to meet with it frequently even amongst a class that has become so numerous as the artistic fraternity in France. I remember an eminent critic who said that when invention was absent from a painting the work had so little interest for him that he did not care to look upon it twice. My own experience has been, rather, that even in the absence of invention there may be certain compensating qualities. One of these is simply refinement of taste, which is enough to make a work attractive when there is no invention whatever, and another is the power of suggesting thoughts and ideas by means of art, a power which may belong to any painter who is himself thoughtful even when he has no inventive genius. There was a picture in the Salon of 1889 by M. Pomey, entitled *Coffee-grinding*, representing a woman with a little coffee-mill, a subject requiring no invention, but elevated in this instance by a perfection of taste in the pose and action of the figure that might have been valuable in the portrait of a great lady. Why should art ever be vulgar? Actions are not vulgar in themselves, they only become so when performed in a vulgar manner. Even a certain rudeness is quite remote from vulgarity when it belongs to the character of the work that has to be done and to the conditions of the surroundings. There was a picture by M. Vail in the Salon of 1888 representing a fisherman at the helm just before tacking. Here he is. Nobody can accuse him of being either elegant, or fashionable, or vulgar. He is doing the plain hard work of seafaring men; and though his oilskin trousers are not exactly a fit (they might do equally well for any man on board), and though his grasp of the tiller is more business-like than refined, still he stands firmly and grandly for what he is, and a king could do no more.

READY ABOUT! BY E. D. VEIL.

Realism without much invention and with perfect good taste in the selection of little-arranged material may be found in the works of several contemporary landscape painters, and particularly in the town landscapes of M. Darien. The example given here is called *Twilight on the Quai Malaquais*, and the drawing, though slight and lacking the colour of

THE MALAQUAIS EMBANKMENT. BY M. DARIEN.

the original picture, perfectly conveys its sentiment. There are, I believe, very few, if any, deviations from truth in the representation of the scene, but there is an exercise of taste and sentiment in the choice of the effect and in the mere placing of the figures. The Quai Malaquais is near the Ecole des Beaux Arts, the bridge in the picture is the Pont du

Carrousel, and the distant pavilion to the right is the Pavillon de Flore of the Tuileries, where Napoleon III. used to have his private cabinet. The picture exactly conveys the impression of Parisian quay scenery so far as a single work could do it. In nature the Parisian embankments are well-known to lovers of the picturesque for their varied effects, especially at sunset and for an hour afterwards.

M. Darien is not the only artist who has found a picturesque interest in Paris without

AVENUE DE LA DEFENSE—NIGHTFALL. BY A. DURST.

exaggerating what happens to be picturesque in some of its features. MM. Leloir, Durst, Manceau, and several others whose names do not occur to me just now, have used Parisian material to convey the most different impressions to the mind. In England Paris is usually thought of as a gay and brilliant city, and no doubt on a fine day, when the trees of the boulevards are freshly green, and the sky is blue above the light tones of the houses, and there is a well-dressed throng on the broad causeways, the place is exhilarating like champagne; but it has other aspects also, and the modern love of veracity in art has led some painters

G

to look for the Paris that is dreary and melancholy, as well as for that which is bright and delightful.   Long streets under snow, with a few pedestrians, a stray dog, or a poor man with a donkey cart, belong in reality just as much to the capital of France as a fashionable boulevard.   Here is a bit of dreary Paris by M. Durst, *Avenue de la Défense —Fin du Jour*.   Those who imagine that Paris, like 'les Polonais' in the song, is 'toujours gai,' may be undeceived by the sadness and dreariness of this picture, which are preserved in this excellent little sketch by the painter himself.

It may be observed that town painters make much of effects of rain, because they afford good opportunities for reflections, and, in fact, turn the asphaltum of the causeways into a

THE HIGHWAY.   BY J. W. RAUGHT.

mirror.   M. Darien, M. Bauré, and others, have taken advantage of these effects, which certainly add a charm to town life in bad weather.   Three or four days before writing this, I was on the Place de la Concorde, all wet in a thaw, and reflecting the glories of a magnificent evening sky, not exactly, but in a fine confusion of colour; and I remembered a picture of the same subject M. Bauré once painted, *La Place Clichy*, with reflections like those on a river.   These reflections have now become one of the properties of the town painter, as they are much more perfect on the modern asphaltum than on anything else.   *Apropos* of roads, there was a curiously interesting picture by M. Raught, an American artist working under French influence, in the Salon of 1889, called simply *La Grande Route*, and representing a broad highway going uphill, the lines of the landscape converging at a farmhouse on the sky-line.   Not a soul visible on the road—'not a cat,' as the French say. The scene was a little discouraging, in consequence of the long climb to be overcome before reaching the top, but it held out a hope for the traveller, though for those who only look at the painted canvas, it must remain for ever unrealised.   It is very easy to imagine the sort of criticism that would have been applied to this picture thirty years ago.   The artist would have been told that he ought to put waggons and horses on his road, and men and women coming from the market; whilst a coarser criticism would have twitted him for having 'lodgings to let.'   There is, at least, this advantage in modern criticism, that it does generally try to understand an artist's motive.   In the present instance, we understand that the road itself, and not wayfarers, is the subject.   The artist has taken a sentimental interest in the road, and though figures are absent from the picture, it is not without a tacit reference to the toils and travels of mankind.*

---

* After the publication of this passage in THE PORTFOLIO, the artist wrote to me to say that I had exactly interpreted his intention.

IV

Impressionism

THE word 'Impressionism' has the usual defect of names intended to be descriptive, in only describing a part of that which it is intended to characterise. It is not possible to convey complicated ideas in a single word, except when the subject is already familiar to the public. Although the principles in question are almost entirely different (having nothing in common but a sincere love of nature), the use of a name reminds one of the English 'Pre-Raphaelitism,' which came to include almost all sincere and downright painting of detail, though much of it was such as no painter existing before the time of Raphael could have practised or even understood. The French Impressionists might argue that there is much more in their doctrine and practice than their title indicates, but the word is useful as a designation, and is so far accurate that it gives an idea of one at least of their principles, especially in landscape-painting.

The first thing to be said about Impressionism is that it need not be considered a novelty, especially by Englishmen. Turner is looked upon as a precursor, the most practical difference between his later and fully emancipated work and that of the modern French Impressionists being that Turner painted in the studio whilst these men work almost exclusively in the open air. Constable, in his sketches, was decidedly an Impressionist, and so have been many more recent artists who are not nominally included in the school. However, the best way to understand the doctrine will be by a fair consideration of the productions that have resulted from it.

One of the earliest of the modern French Impressionists was Edouard Manet, whose premature death prevents me from speaking of his work as belonging to the artistic production of the present day, though it is impossible to overlook it in the history of the sect, and, indeed, the living Impressionists still affectionately consider Manet one of themselves : ' he, being dead, yet speaketh.' The example that he set was one of perfect honesty, absolute faith in his principles, and a too complete confidence in his own powers. He had deep convictions about veracity, and staked upon them the whole success of his career. Being independent in fortune, he was never compelled to adapt his talents to the taste of others, and he never made any concessions either to popular or to more cultivated tastes. One of his earliest admirers, M. Zola, admitted that he ' painted neither history nor the soul, that what is called composition did not exist for him.' Then M. Zola went on to say, ' He treats his figure-pictures as it is permitted in the schools to treat pictures of still life ; I mean that he groups his models rather accidentally, and that all his care afterwards is to fix them on the canvas as he sees them, with the vigorous oppositions by which they detach themselves one from another.' If this account of Manet's practice is true (and Zola knew him well), is it not an admission that he worked rather by the eye than by the mind—that there was neither thought nor composition in his work, but observation only ? In execution, Manet's work was an improvisation in the presence of nature, and who can count upon the regularity in the action of high artistic faculties that would be necessary to maintain a steady excellence in improvisation ? It is a fact that the quality of Manet's painting was very unequal, especially in the texture and colouring of flesh. However, the absolute sincerity of it gave a claim to serious consideration, and the artist's resolute study of nature endowed it with novelty and freshness. M. Zola spoke of him repeatedly as an 'analyst,' but in my view his work was rather synthetic than analytic, and I notice that those writers who are now most in sympathy with the Impressionists, and most directly inspired by them, use the words 'synthesis' and 'synthetic' as being the aim and the characteristic of their art. Like some other French artists of our time, Manet had a way of translating old themes by modern examples. In this way some of his pictures, that were considered coarse, vulgar, and even immoral, were merely experiments in the modernisation of Dutch and Italian themes that no one ever objects to in the old masters.

A name which by its resemblance to that of Manet has sometimes created confusion, even in print, is that of Claude Monet, the Impressionist landscape-painter. It is natural that the principles of the sect should have been applied to a department of art in which the variety of effects and their fugitive character seem enough to suggest the practice, if they do not formulate the doctrine, of Impressionism.

A VILLAGE BY THE SEINE. BY C. MONET.

What, indeed, would be the ideally best way of painting a landscape? What, in the artistic sense, *is* a natural landscape? Is it a tangible substance, such as granite and oak, or is it an effect of colour and light? The answer is, that although tangible substances exist in landscape they do not make the *scene*, which is the result of effect as much as of substance, being a synthesis of the two, and that landscape-painting ought to give this synthesis. When from theory we come to practice, we find that effects are fugitive, and require very summary treatment if they are to be painted at all from nature, or even whilst they remain fresh in the memory. M. Claude Monet works exclusively from nature, and this has two consequences: the first, that a large proportion of his pictures remain unfinished and are never shown to anybody; the second, that in those he exhibits, the substance of the landscape, the material part of it, is often dealt with in such a summary fashion that trees and houses are given in a sort of shorthand. The rapid transience of natural effects must always either hurry the artist so as to make quiet work impossible for him, or else compel him to paint from memory. M. Monet accepts heroically the inconveniences of working from nature. His constant study of natural effects has produced in his mind a complete divergence from those ideas about landscape colour which are born and bred in studios in great cities. The city painter fancies that nature is grey or brown, with a little dull green on grass, or permissible pale blue in the sky towards the top of the picture. M. Monet has seen the real colouring of nature—seas of sapphire and emerald, or dark purple and violet far away, cliffs of brilliant white or stained with reds incredible to the citizen critic, and confused medleys of the richest colours in weedy pools upon the sands. He has seen the Atlantic waves beat wildly on the purple rocks of Brittany; he has studied the Mediterranean, with its pale, pure blues and greens, dark by comparison with the sun-baked fortifications of Antibes and the aërial radiance of the distant maritime Alps. For variety of observation, joined to complete singleness of purpose in each separate work, no French landscape-painter is comparable to Claude Monet. The utmost dreariness of a frozen river and a snowed-up little town in Normandy, the summer glory of the south, the burning autumnal foliage by some quiet trout-stream in contrast with the persistent green of its grassy bank, are all equally interesting to this open-minded observer; and each separate phase of nature that he represents occupies him exclusively at the time, so that there is never any confusion in his mind between one motive and another. Yet for many years Monet has been a most unpopular artist, and his unpopularity has been due both to his merits and his defects. First, he sees and imitates natural colour (including even the bluish or violet shadows in landscape), colour that always puzzles and amazes the unobservant ; and he tries to raise the key of his tonality as high as he can towards the exalted pitch of natural light — two endeavours that are sure to make pictures look glaring, especially whilst the paint is fresh. In colour and light Claude Monet does not paint what other people expect or want to see, but tries for what he has himself seen in nature. Next, he has the purest possible landscape instinct, not seeking much or often for adventitious human interest, as the old masters always did, and as prudent moderns have done generally. A lonely place is interesting for him if it has natural beauty or character—or even an effect may make it interesting. Now, as to imperfections, although M. Monet is said by his friends to be a good draughtsman when he chooses, he puts very little drawing into his painting ; he is not half so sensitive to the beauty of form which exists in natural landscape as he is to its glory of colour and brilliance of light, and for those who love the delicate beauty of form, this inattention to it is vexatious. The desire for broad truth of colour and effect has caused M. Monet to pass over natural detail, which has an infinite charm for many who love nature as sincerely as he does himself but in a different way. Finally, and this perhaps is the gravest of M. Monet's deficiencies or indifferences, he seems wholly indifferent to the charm of composition. Surely this is a misfortune, or else (if the result of obedience to a principle) a mistake. I suspect that M. Monet rejects composition from a sort of misplaced honesty : 'The place was like that, and I had no right to alter it ;' or, as a realist once said for a too overwhelming cloud in one of his drawings, 'I am not answerable for the cloud —it was *there*.' These principles would be excellent in legal testimony, but they are the negation of art. The charm of composition is as delightful, though not so absolutely essential, in painting as in music. It is said that M. Monet and the other French Impressionists are great admirers of Turner ; if so, they surely must have noticed that he composed always. Setting aside studies of separate objects, intended for his private use, there is not a picture nor a drawing by Turner that is not com-

A COASTGUARDSMAN'S HUT. BY C. MONET.

posed like a piece of music. It seems to me that M. Monet, in his praiseworthy devotion to Nature, has placed himself needlessly in a position of antagonism to Art, and that this may account for much of his unpopularity, though some of it is simply due to his life in the open air, a kind of life that produces eccentricity in landscape-painters. The best rules for them, if they wish to escape from eccentricity, are to paint always in a studio in the middle of a great, gloomy, capital city, to avoid Nature, and to study the oldest and brownest pictures they can find.

The ancient conflict between synthesis and analysis in painting may be settled by saying that analysis is necessary in early study and natural in primitive art, but that all advanced art is founded upon synthesis. The Impressionists and their friends have often affirmed that their art is purely synthetic, and does not pretend to be anything else. They claim to see and represent visible nature as a whole—at least, what strikes them at once, form and effect together. When applied to the figure, this principle is incompatible with any special insistence on the line, so that according to it the painting of Ingres, for example, would be comparatively primitive, however able in its own way. Amongst contemporary Frenchmen, M. Albert Besnard is, perhaps, the artist who has made the most curious experiments in effect. In the Universal Exhibition there was a picture by him of a naked female figure warming herself at a fire. It was amazing at first, on account of the contrast of coloured lights, yet on further acquaintance it appeared to be nothing more than an 'impression' of the figure painted on Turnerian principles, and with colouring, too, that bore a strange resemblance to Turner's experiments with yellow, red, and blue, in hot and cold opposition. M. Besnard paints effect portraits also in which the sitter becomes the victim of the light. M. Renoir, one of the most powerful of the Impressionists, painted a remarkable portrait of Madame Samary, the well-known laughing actress whom Paris regretted ; and not only did that portrait recall Turner's colour, it also reminded one of some peculiar qualities in his execution, especially its visionary gradations and evanescence. When a painter, having a sitter before him, determines to paint the effect and not the substance, he may almost lose the sense of substance, and so reach a kind of ideal in which the human form and flesh become, as it were, sublimated into a spiritual vision. Remembering well the real Samary, who had nothing ghostly about her, I felt before Renoir's portrait as if the painter had seen her not in this world, nor yet in any dreary region of the dead, but in some cheerful elysium of light and colour adapted to her merry and kindly genius.

The same M. Renoir is the painter of many other works which give evidence of a strong natural gift for colour along with a certain rashness so far as the public is concerned. These painters feel themselves to be in a condition of antagonism to the world around them that leads to self-assertion, and is, therefore, not wholly favourable to their art. M. Renoir sees that nature is not all brown and grey ; he sees both violet and green, which used to be almost forbidden colours in the French school, and he is disposed to paint every hue up to its full pitch of chromatic intensity. One proof of his enjoyment of bright hues may be found in his studies of flowers, which have, no doubt, influenced his other work. Monet, also, has painted flowers in their full natural colours for decorative purposes. M. Renoir's colouring must be looked upon as a sort of *défi* by partisans of the old French brown and grey. His important picture of boating men and girls refreshing themselves by the Seine (in the private collection of M. Durand Ruel) is full of healthy flesh-colouring, remote indeed from the cadaverous skins that have been common in earthy and bituminous art. Besides healthy colouring there is strong human character in M. Renoir's work : his young people and children are especially characteristic. Still, with all his gifts, one sees that he has been fighting a battle, as our own Pre-Raphaelites did in their time of conflict, and the combative spirit is never the best for art : a happy serenity is best for it. M. Renoir is not alone in this combativeness ; it is visible in other Impressionists by their resolute refusal of concession to all established ideas about taste. There is M. Forain, for example, a draughtsman of great gifts in the way of memory and observation, with a surprising knowledge of character and a most incisive and laconic way of expressing it— evidently, in short, a man of genius and painter as well as draughtsman. This year M. Forain had a picture of a provincial racecourse in the exhibition of the Rue de Sèze, showing talent, of course, but so oddly composed as to throw most of the interest up towards the top of the canvas, whilst a quarter of it was an unfurnished space of green. The old dread of unfurnished spaces does not seem to trouble these painters of the present day. M. Montenard, another Impressionist, has exhibited two views near Toulon, representing the intense glare of southern light on spaces of dusty road or baked hillside, and he is satisfied with taking you there and leaving you without shelter from the pitiless blaze. Certainly nobody before the present generation ever made one feel so strongly the fierce climate of Provence. Claude's sunshine is mildly agreeable, and that of Turner is English and foggy, but M. Montenard's sunshine has the steady southern intensity—you know that it will go on without a cloud till the stars shine in the sultry night. Other modern Frenchmen are grappling with the sunshine difficulty : one in the Roman summer, another in the Algerian desert, and several, like M. Point and M. Dinet, are trying to solve the problem of sunshine on the naked figure. M. Point exhibits in 1891, under the title *Caresse de Soleil*, a study of a girl going to bathe. She is in the full glare, and by reflections and transparence the artist has contrived to express light without losing flesh-colour ; but when he tries to carry the greens of vegetation up to the required pitch they lose half their colour in mere whiteness. This is the old difficulty, the combination of full light with adequate colour, and the resources of art are not enough to overcome it. Some Impressionists more prudently confine themselves, like M. Dannat, to sober hues and a moderate light—to black, to quiet greys, and ochrous tints of red or yellow—all which by a due choice of materials and effect may be as strictly true as the brightest colouring of Monet or the strongest sunshine of Montenard. Another painter who is classed amongst the Impressionists, M. Eugène Boudin, is a quiet colourist, not because he works below the

truth of nature, but because he seems usually to select, by preference, those effects that allow an artist to remain within the limits of what is unobtrusive — in M. Boudin's case chiefly greys, varied by pale blues and cool sea-greens. He permits himself an occasional touch of brighter colour, usually in the paint of some vessel, where the cruder taste of the ship-painter affords an excuse for a stronger green or red, which the artist harmonises as he likes and modifies by

THE BANKS OF THE SEYNE. BY MONTENARD.

distance and effect. M. Boudin is not a young artist, though classed with the new school. He was born in 1825, and I am not aware that he has ever worked on any other principles than that of simple fidelity to his impressions, and to this he still adheres. His knowledge of the sea and shipping is of the familiar kind which may belong to one born and bred on the Atlantic shore of France, and who has lived with nature for forty years, troubling himself very little about artistic movements in the capital, and remaining till comparatively late in life in a position of obscurity not unfavourable to the honest craft of a sincere marine-painter, whose business is with boats and fisher-folk rather than with fashionable society. M. Boudin knows the sea (I mean the sea of the Channel), and those who get their living by it, as Millet knew the fields and the peasantry, except that in Millet's work the human element was more important and the landscape counted for less. I may add that M. Boudin has much unobtrusive manual skill, the result of long and constant practice, and that he does not seem to be a militant painter, inclined to take the offensive against public taste, but works on independently, in complete indifference to it, loving his waves and fishing-boats, and his distant gleams of light on restless pale-green seas. His artistic ancestry has been traced by a French critic to the old Dutch marine-painters, probably with reason. There is no striking novelty in his art, and it may be overlooked for its absence of pretension ; but it is fresh, lively, and sincere, besides being grounded on an adequate observation of nature.

If painting is a difficult art, criticism is not quite so easy as the old French proverb represents it.   One of the principal difficulties of criticism lies in that very partiality of taste and expression which constitutes the personal interest of the fine arts.   Every painter has his own peculiar view of nature and his own peculiar tolerance of materials or appearances that seem objectionable to others.   It is, therefore, not always easy for a critic to tune his own mind into unison with the mind of a painter who feels quite differently from himself.   There is M. Camille Pissarro, who has some very ardent admirers, and yet who is very foreign to me.   I do not enter into his ideas of composition, or follow him easily in his selection of materials.   It seems to me that he admits lines and masses that a stricter taste would alter or avoid, and that he includes objects that a more scrupulous artist would reject.   This, perhaps, may be in accordance with the Impressionist faith ; if so, it is an additional reason for disliking the sectarian spirit in art.   Even in Daubigny's river landscapes, not to speak of Turner's, we find a sense of enjoyment when the line of shore is beautiful, and a delight in the happy situation of some old French town that comes in exactly where it ought to be.   In M. Pissarro's work we have Nature's own indifference to these things.   He does not seem to care whether the line of shore is beautiful or not, and he has so little objection to ugly objects that in one of his pictures the tower of a distant cathedral is nearly obliterated by a long chimney and the smoke or steam that issues from it, whilst there are other long chimneys close to the cathedral, just as they might present themselves in a photograph. By this needless degree of fidelity M. Pissarro loses one of the great advantages of painting. He would probably answer, that topographic accuracy is not his object, but that he remains faithful to his impressions, whatever they may happen to include.   His real source of inspiration is the love of light ; he does not paint the incidence of light on objects with any scientific precision, but has a synthetic conception of light permeating landscape, and his works are undeniably luminous.   They are also perfectly harmonious in the key chosen, as, for example, this quiet sketch of a woman sewing, which is more easily reproduced than a sunny landscape.

WOMAN SEWING.

An Impressionist who, so far as I know his work, gives me unfailing satisfaction is M. Dauphin.   He paints water admirably, whether in stormy waves that break on a Mediterranean shore during the mistral, or in long trailing reflections in a sheltered harbour like the port of Toulon, which has afforded him material for more than one brilliant and interesting picture.   All his work seems to be frank, fresh, and observant, and though he admits colours which exist in nature, but which the narrowness of the old criticism forbade in art, and the timidity of the old landscape-painters shrank from representing, I do not perceive in M. Dauphin any of that rashness in colouring that comes from a spirit of protest or defiance ; he is simply observant and independent. Again, his execution is remarkably straightforward ; his touches are laid in their places and never disturbed afterwards, yet at the same time there is no bravura, no false excitement in his execution, as there is, for example, sometimes in that of the Swedish Impressionist, Zorn.

This decision of handling appears to be a virtue that the Impressionists cultivate with a special intention—and certainly it *is* a virtue. It becomes a vice only when the decision is that of pretentious ignorance, which can never be the case with a student of nature like M. Dauphin.

The first impression produced by the paintings of M. Degas is that their extreme originality is due to wilful eccentricity, but a more accurate account of them might be that they are the result of observation independent of other art. M. Degas sees human nature in his own way, and describes it with a candour that must be shocking to people who have any illusions left. It has been said of a certain class of his works that they represent men and women, especially women, as if they did not know that they were watched. The artist seems like an invisible spirit, malicious rather than discreet, who can pass through keyholes or partition-walls, whilst nothing betrays his presence. He is a most expressive character-draughtsman, a close observer of attitude, and pitiless in his revelation of bodily imperfection. He refuses obedience to the maxim, 'Toute vérité n'est pas bonne à dire.' Some pictures of his give plain evidence of a serious study of colour. I do not know enough of them to set any limits to the artist's experiments, but suppose that his chief interest is in the study of quiet tones, and in harmonies or contrasts not too obvious to the multitude. In landscape he is extremely realist ; perhaps if I said he had no sense of beauty or the ideal, he would answer that he saw beauty and ideality where I am incapable of seeing them. However this may be, it seems to me that his choice of material (if it is a choice) is commonplace, but that his painting is not commonplace.

It is impossible in this brief notice to mention all the Impressionists who have won some degree of reputation, but it would be wrong to omit M. Sisley. In some of his works he is nearer to Claude Monet than others, but he has his own originality.*

HAYMAKING. BY A. SISLEY.

Like Monet, he does not shrink from the frankness of natural colour, and from the unexpected oppositions that it offers ; yet in some of his works—as, for example, a broadly picturesque sketch of Moret, with its church and houses, bridge and river — he has sought unity of colour rather than any surprise of contrast, which leads one to the remark that in Impressionism there may be several distinct tendencies. In Claude Monet the protest is in favour of what seems strange and heterodox in natural colour and light ; in Degas the protest is in behalf of neglected characteristics and the commonplace formerly condemned as prosaic ; in Renoir it is in behalf of colour, in Camille Pissarro for the diffusion of light ; but whatever may be the object aimed at, there is always in these men some special interest in Nature that justifies, in their view, a revolt against the traditions of Art. No one can see more clearly than I do that the products of such revolts are but partial successes, that they have never the completeness only attainable in tranquillity when there is no antagonism ; yet these movements of rebellion in favour of Nature are the refreshment of Art itself, like waters brought from a distant lake or river to the heart of some populous city, some dingy Glasgow, some thirsty and sunburnt Marseilles.

---

* The little *croquis* given above as an illustration is extremely hasty and slight, but it contains as many truths as could well be set down on paper in the very short time given to it. A sketch of this kind is completely synthetic and suggestive of many things at once in its swift shorthand. I give it as an example of the Impressionist way of taking very rapid notes from nature.

V

The Survival of Classical Sentiment

THE best chance for a sentiment to be genuine is that nobody should be compelled to profess it. In literature, a language that we love is usually one that we have studied of our own account, and the poetry that is most enjoyed is that which has not yet been imposed upon us in school-books. There is a rebellious element in our nature, and especially in the artistic and critical part of it, which lives in secret revolt against the pedagogue who tells us what to admire, and which goes for its private pleasure to sources that he has not indicated. There was a time, lasting well into the nineteenth century, when a sort of classicism was imposed upon all students of literature and art, and the effect of it was to impel many of them to seek intellectual pleasures in almost anything that promised emancipation. At the present day the deliverance is complete so far as liberty of doctrine is concerned. We may be classical, romantic, realist, anything that we like; and the effect of this emancipation has not been to destroy the classical spirit, but to give it a fresh vitality in new forms. If an artist is classical in these days, it is because he has the genuine sentiment, and just because the sentiment is genuine it reveals itself in personal and peculiar ways, unlike what any authoritative classical teacher would have prescribed for it.

The vast mural painting by M. Puvis de Chavannes in the new amphitheatre of the Sorbonne, is an excellent example of the genuineness of the classical sentiment that survives at the present day. The work is as modern as possible, yet it is connected with antiquity, not by obedience to an ancient authority felt to be foreign, but by the effects of assimilation. I happened to be looking at this remarkable performance with an eminent French artist, and he said, 'The picture seems like a revelation of ancient art : the Greeks must have painted so.' The technical execution of a Greek wall-painting would probably have been different, because this work is in oil with a dull surface, and we believe that the Greeks employed distemper, protected afterwards by varnish; but in one quality this work may be a renewal of antique art, and that is in its elevation of idea and its complete detachment from the actual. Before going into the details of the allegorical intention, we feel that it admits us into a world which is not ours, a world of serene dignity, as of souls in a sacred garden occupied with grave and noble meditations. Even the landscape, majestically beautiful, is hardly terrestrial. It is in that land of poetry and allegory where the light is not of the sun, and the colour is an imagined harmony of pale hues. We learn from the inscription that the central personage is the Sorbonne; that other figures represent Eloquence, Poetry, Youth that drinks of knowledge, and Age with trembling hands. The great central compartment is divided from the side compartments by two trees.* To the left, the lateral composition represents Philosophy and History, with the contest between Spiritualism and Materialism, and Archaeology examining the *débris* of the past. The composition on the right is devoted to Science. One might easily criticise the allegorical conception on the ground of a certain

---

* The central compartment is the only one indicated in the accompanying sketch from the original cartoon.

incongruity.   Material realities, such as the land and the sea, are personified along with special sciences, such as botany and geology, whilst geometry is not represented by a figure but by a group of students, and electricity is a flame carried by a youth.   It is odd to see two such different ideas as Spiritualism and the Sorbonne, a doctrine and a teaching and examining college, represented by two female figures.   Perhaps it is better not to trouble ourselves too much with the allegory, which serves as a pretext for a work of this kind. This vast composition is successful as a piece of noble and serious decoration, which is enough. I may add that it harmonises admirably with the minor decorative work that accompanies it in the magnificent amphitheatre of the Sorbonne.   One does not look for the imitation of nature in such a composition as this, but for the artistic unity of a great scheme in which the painter's will and idea are throughout indisputably predominant.   The painter has been roughly criticised for want of refinement in drawing and for falsity in colour ; but this is pre-eminently one of those cases to which the wise defence, 'Had it been better it would have been worse,' is most applicable.   There are several French artists who can draw an outline

FROM A MURAL PAINTING.   BY M. PUVIS DE CHAVANNES.

with much elegance and precision ; but if the quality of their drawing could be added, by way of correction, to this work, it would ruin it by the addition of a minor and unnecessary order of beauty beneath the gravity of this noble form of art.   And as for colour, the colouring here is decorative and takes only just so much of nature as the artist cares to have. To ask for complete truth, or for more subordination to nature, is to misapprehend the object of decorative painting.

The entire mass of French work from the nude figure is connected directly with classical studies as painters understand them—that is, with the study of antique sculpture and drawing, and with the painting of the Italian Renaissance.   The painter of rustic figures may look to contemporary life and forget antiquity as completely as a modern novelist, but he who attempts the nude is led back irresistibly to classical times and becomes more or less imbued with classical ideas.   A sort of gentle Paganism pervades all that section of the French school which still concerns itself with the beauty of the body.   According to the student's estimate, this is of all subjects the most serious, because it most requires the long labours of the *atelier*, but the outer aspect of the art produced is usually either dreamy or frivolous. The poetic minds go back to a Pagan dream, the prosaic ones fall into frivolous details of the bedchamber and the bathroom.   The sympathies of the higher criticism must here be entirely with the Pagans.   They do at least preserve us from a realism that easily borders upon indecency. M. Franc Lamy is a devoted student of the nude who enjoys the contrast of it with landscape, especially with the beauty of the woods; and so he imagines for himself a poetical woodland world, whose inhabitants are all of the female sex and almost unacquainted with the use of clothes—a sunny and a flowery land of idleness, with quiet ponds to bathe in, and grassy lawns to lounge upon, and never a prying eye to disturb the serene equanimity of the beautiful human animals that dwell therein. It is a Paradise before the Fall, with a plurality of Eves and neither a serpent nor an Adam. The birds are doves that fear no falcon, the season summer that will never give place to winter, the time of life is youth.

Another inventor of prettiness is M. Aubert, who is closely in sympathy with classical feeling, and, having a touch of humour, amuses himself and us with playful fancies about little Loves and girls who guard them, or meet them unexpectedly, or take them to be sold in the market. In one picture (1885) Aurora trims the wings of Love as he stands on the rocky margin of a rivulet—a pretty fancy very gracefully realised. All these pictures are essentially French in conception, with little more than an allusion to antiquity; and though

THE END OF SUMMER. BY R. COLLIN.

they seem pretty trifles almost without thought, they are not without some novelty and originality of invention. It is a common mistake to undervalue this light kind of art because the ideas expressed in it are unimportant, yet the training required for it is at least as serious as that of the historical painter. An artist of M. Bouguereau's experience in religious painting finds in *The Disarming of Cupid* a subject diffi‑ cult enough to tax his strength, though the figures are but a young woman and a little boy. One of the most important pictures by the same artist in the Universal Exhibition of 1889 was his great composition of *The Youth of Bacchus;* and in the Salon of the same year, Carolus Duran exhibited an important bacchanalian picture representing the god sitting on his chariot and drawn by serving-men, whilst he is followed by a crowd of revellers. This work was conceived more in the spirit of the Renaissance than in that of Greek antiquity; it was composed in well-massed groups, full of movement, and afforded the painter a good opportunity for displaying his mastery of flesh in the often-sought contrast between fair women and sun-browned men. The real motive of such works as the two just mentioned is the interest of a trial of strength with the old masters. A modern painter reaches great executive ability, feels that he has powers of invention, and is attracted to bacchanalian subjects because Rubens painted them, but they hardly belong to our age. The genuine and unaffected classicism of our time is either dreamy and fanciful, or else an archaeological attempt to resuscitate antique life. There was a picture in the Salon of 1890, by M. Gaston Bussière, which was entitled *La Gloire.* In a dreamy landscape, on the banks of a melancholy stream, a poet is lying with his head in the lap of a maiden, his lyre having dropped from the dead hand, whilst a stately draped figure advances slowly towards him, bringing the laurel crown too late. Here the pictorial conception and treatment are purely classical, yet the motive is modern— it belongs to the artist, and does not set up any contest with the great men of the Renaissance. So it is with the delicate and charming pictures by R. Collin, such as *The End of Summer,* in the Salon of 1888, and *Youth,* exhibited in the following year. The first was intended for a decorative panel, and represented a woodland landscape with girls dancing on an open sward. Another girl in the foreground comes towards the spectator with her arms full of plants that she has gathered. The attraction of a work of this quality (which, as with all poetical works, increases on further acquaintance) is due to its ideality, which is classical, and not remote from that of Corot. This is equivalent to saying that it is at the same time French and connected with a close observation of nature. The other picture, *Youth*, is an idyll of very early rustic love. A shepherd boy, stretched upon the grass, is kissing a young shepherdess on the tip of her chin—a liberty that she does not resent, but permits with a certain natural gravity and decorum. They have not much clothing, yet they have a little, and it is not cold in the land of idyllic poetry. There was a beautiful moderation in the painter's treatment of the incompletely developed forms. The accompanying very slight sketch from a picture called *Adolescence*, exhibited by the same artist in 1890, gives evidence of what seems to me the admirable negative quality of not seeking for beauty out of place. The sketch is delightfully simple and harmonious; the artist has not given the subject the least addition of a beauty that did not properly belong to it, yet the result is essentially classical.

ADOLESCENCE. BY R. COLLIN.

The mere naming of pictures may sometimes be a misfortune, as it may, in itself, be the only cause of discord or incompatibility between the expectations awakened in our minds and the work that ought to satisfy them. M. Falguière exhibited in the Salon of 1889 a study of the nude, which was creditable simply as a study from a rather slight and insignificant model, not by any means representative either of opulent physical beauty or of superior mental force. The model had posed with one hand on her hip and the other raised to the back of her head, one foot on the ground and the other on a step, as if descending a staircase. There was no harm so far; but, unluckily, the artist called his model *Juno*, put a cloud behind her, and a peacock, and poised her in front of a precipice as she descended into a rocky dell. The title immediately required more than what was given; it required the utmost expression of feminine authority.

As Juno should be a great Queen, so Venus ought at least to be a beautiful woman. In 1890 there was a Venus by M. Lemaire standing on a dolphin, and holding out her long tresses—a very straight and tall person, but not in the least seductive, and more like the personification of Moral Superiority than of Woman's dangerous power over men. The picture, nevertheless, was admirably and truly classical in the sentiment of the Renaissance, and would have served effectually as a part of some noble decoration.

M. Jules Lefebvre has, I think, been uniformly successful in his classical pictures, and the reason I take to be the union, in his case, of a fine taste with sufficient imagination and sympathy to throw himself heartily into the spirit of antique legend. I do not know any modern classical work more perfectly successful than *Psyche*. She is sitting on a rock in hell with the box in her hand that Venus gave her, and that Proserpine filled with mephitic vapour. She has not yet opened the box, but is looking wearily on the black infernal sky and the gloomy waters. The enduring charm of that beautiful tale about

Psyche is that it suggests so many interpretations. One that occurs to us in the presence of M. Lefebvre's picture is the hard situation of mental beauty in the dark and rude environment of a lower world. The sky may be black, the waters gloomy and deep, the rocks pitiless, yet Psyche, sad as she is, has still a star upon her forehead.

The same painter had a lighter and less significant, but equally classical, picture in the Salon of 1887, *Morning Glory*, of which we are able to give a sketch. The same classical culture is visible in pictures by Lefebvre which have no connexion with antique subjects—in fact, it permeates all his work ; but he has sometimes painted important mythological compositions, as, for example, the beautifully composed *Surprise of Diana* in the Salon of 1879—a lesson to some artists of the extremely modern school, who reject composition altogether.

MORNING GLORY. BY LEFEBVRE.

Another eminent painter whose mind is naturally classical is M. Henner. He has the antique love of simplicity in subject with the preference for the nude, and a willingness to remain satisfied with few colours and a few strong, plain oppositions, hardly more complicated than the black and white, or the red and black, on ancient vases. The element in M. Henner's taste which is not antique is his love for extreme softness and vagueness of contour, which he may have learned from the ripest Italian art. It is curious that a painter who has so little to say, whose subjects are usually confined to one or two figures doing nothing in particular, should be always interesting, yet he undoubtedly is so by the essentially artistic nature of his conceptions. There is his *Eclogue*, for instance, painted in 1879, with one female figure leaning on the edge of a well, and another sitting on the grass playing on a pipe, her long hair trailing behind her to the ground. The landscape is a dark, dense wood, a gleam of a pond, a bit of ordinary hill, and a limited space of sky. Yet, notwithstanding the absence of detail, the work is so complete, so harmonious, and its few masses so well ordered, that one asks for nothing more. In 1880 a famous picture by M. Henner represented a nude female figure with her knee on the stone edge of a well or basin as she looks down into the water, her hair falling in a great mass against the usual mass of sombre foliage. Intellectually a picture of this kind is nothing, artistically it leaves nothing to be desired. So with the *Weeping Nymph* of 1884, a girl kneeling, or sitting on her heels, the head bowed forward, the face hidden in her hands, and again the same opposition of flesh against dark twilight foliage. These are not exactly recent instances, but Henner is always the same, always satisfied with the same few notes of colour and chiaroscuro, meaning little, yet exquisitely attuned and performed with a 'virtuosité' in its own way unsurpassed. And this satisfaction with few and simple ideas, perfectly expressed, I take to be the special mark of the classical genius.

Of all contemporary French painters, the one who is most in harmony with antiquity itself, and who most constantly dwells upon it, is M. Hector Le Roux. From the very beginning of his career, some years before the Franco-German war, M. Le Roux began to live in the life and poetry of the ancients, and having himself a delicate poetic sense, he produced works which, if they did not become popular in the vulgar sense of the word, assured for him the respectful attention of the more cultivated French critics. He has never worked for effect, never attempted to draw attention to himself by those displays which are the common resource of the self-advertiser, and it is not probable that he will ever have the sort of success that makes a name known to all sorts of people ; but if refined visitors to the Salons ever miss his works, it can only be by accident. His colour is usually pale and delicate, and he does not care for those strong oppositions of light and dark that are always present in the works of Henner, besides which his figures are usually draped, and he enjoys the beauty of draperies almost as a Greek sculptor might have enjoyed them. The subjects chosen by M. Le Roux are sometimes from the beliefs of the ancients and sometimes from their daily life. The picture entitled *Brother and Sister*, of which a sketch is given here, is supposed to be an example of antique portraiture, and gains a little additional interest from this make-belief. M. Le Roux exhibited in 1883 *The Sacrarium*, or holy place in an antique dwelling, and in another

BROTHER AND SISTER. BY LE ROUX.

Salon a *Sleeping Vestal*, both pictures strongly imbued with a respect for past sanctities. M. Le Roux has not that strong realism which gives such a peculiar interest to the restoration of antique life by Mr. Alma Tadema, his art is more a poetical souvenir of a vanished past than an actual realisation of it. A more powerful but much less refined artist, M. Boulanger, often realised very powerfully certain episodes of life in ancient Rome, as, for example, a brutal dealer in slaves, stuffing his mouth as he exhibits his unfortunate merchandise. A well-known picture by M. Boulanger, entitled *The Mother of the Gracchi*, was exhibited in 1885. She is coming down steps with her two boys, one on each side, looking proud and happy, but with an intensely French expression on her face. Quite recently M. Rochegrosse, without imitating antique art, has given a glimpse of private life in Rome in his *Quail-fight*, which takes place on a table with a family sitting round and looking on. It does not follow that because ancient life is vividly represented, there is anything of the classical spirit in the representation. A good deal of the painting that illustrates Greece and Rome is merely modern *genre* painting employing itself on other subjects. On the other hand, there may be much of the antique spirit in works that have no direct reference to antiquity. I have noticed this in some pictures by M. Munier, especially his *Guardian Angels* in the Salon of 1890, and a charming domestic scene in that of 1889, where a little boy

SPRING. BY MANGEANT.

was being dressed — a work most classical in sentiment and taste, yet absolutely modern at the same time. The sentiment of a picture called *Spring*, exhibited by M. Mangeant in 1887, was also classical, but rather of the early Renaissance than derived directly from antiquity.

As for the permeating influence of the classical spirit in the treatment of purely modern subjects, it is an interesting matter of investigation for a critic, but the reader would not thank me for dwelling upon it, and these things cannot be explained without very numerous illustrations. It is enough to say that although classicism does not survive as an exclusive dogma, it still survives as an active influence in culture, lending to many works a charm of elegance and taste that we seldom meet with in those from which it is altogether absent.

VI

Historical Genre

THE title of this chapter may seem contradictory, especially to readers who are acquainted with the definition of *genre* given in the best French dictionaries. They tell us that *genre*, in painting, includes all kinds of subjects except history and landscape, whilst my title may seem to confound history with something else. I find it convenient because, in fact, the painters of historical *genre* do mix together history and the observation of ordinary life. Their object is to make historical subjects lively and interesting, and they attain this by giving a play of character, often in quite subordinate personages who are supernumeraries, and always by transferring to a past age the results of their observation of the present. The device is by no means new, but it may be doubted whether the kind of art that is here called 'historical *genre*' has ever been so successfully cultivated as at the present day. Contemporary painters are so well acquainted with the costumes and other belongings of past times, and so observant of human nature in the present, that a clever mixture of the two produces the illusion of actuality far better than it could ever be produced by historical painting of a formal and dignified kind.

Amongst the younger French artists of the present day, those in the prime of life and in the full energy of production, it would be difficult to mention one more completely representative than M. François Flameng. His interest in the past differs from that of the ordinary archaeologist or historian in its extreme vivacity. The past is always alive for him, and not only his favourite century, which seems to be the eighteenth, but other centuries also, whenever his attention is directed to them by the exigencies of the task before him. The word 'task,' in his case, appears to be almost inapplicable, as, although unsparing of labour, he finds everything a labour of love. A curious and fortunate peculiarity of his organization is that scale of execution is indifferent to him. He will turn from a tiny canvas, finished like a miniature, to a mural painting thirty feet long, without more embarrassment than Nature herself appears to feel when she builds the skeletons of a mouse and an elephant. Few artists have been so fortunate in their studies and in their gifts. The son of a distinguished engraver, who was nearer to painters than any other of his time, young Flameng lived from childhood in the world of art, and received nothing but encouragement and help. Having gained at the Lycée Louis le Grand, a sufficient scholastic training to place literary studies within his reach, he left before it had become too late to make himself an artist, and studied under Cabanel. After exhibiting a few early pictures, especially *The Lectern*, which immediately attracted attention, he became famous in 1879 with his *Appel des Girondins*. The scene is in the prison of the Conciergerie on the morning when they were called forth to execution, after passing the night there. They had eaten their last meal together, encouraging each other, and talking of death and a future state. After the *Appel* they were taken together in carts to the scaffold, where their twenty-one heads were cut off in twenty-eight minutes. In the picture the meal is just over, and the emissary of the revolutionary tribunal is reading the warrant. The variety and intensity of expression in the faces and attitudes, the strength of individual character in all the figures, and the complete pictorial unity of the work, made it one of the most striking and most easily remembered pictures of modern times. It gained the 'Prix du Salon' and placed its author in the first rank amongst the younger artists. Instead, however, of settling down to repeat revolutionary subjects, he went to Italy to study the great masters, chiefly the Florentines, and since then has divided his time amongst works of the most various character, including great mural pictures, highly finished cabinet pictures, and everything between them.

An indefatigable worker, François Flameng has avoided the danger of swift production by a constant attention to every necessary or significant detail, so that he is not only one of the most rapid of painters but also one of the most accurate. A great part of his well-deserved success is due to the individuality and character that he puts into every figure, even in those compositions where the figures are most numerous. It is so, of course, with the personages in our illustrations. How much character there is in the two chess-players and in the lady who is looking on! One cannot say much for her way of holding herself;

AT THE LECTERN. BY F. FLAMENG.

her attitude, like her dress, belongs to that state which our fathers called 'dishabille,' but how natural she is, and how feminine! Observe especially the pretty hands, posed just as they should be without a thought. In this picture, and in many others by the same painter, there is an ingredient of quiet humour, whilst in such serious pictures as the *Appel des Girondins*, humour is only banished to make way for a pervading sense of tragedy.

In pictures neither humorous nor tragic, such as the large decorative paintings in the grand staircase at the Sorbonne, M. Flameng's object has simply been to give life to the past, and in this he has been eminently successful. Whoever they are— Etienne Dolet, Jacques Amyot, Ronsard, Clement Marot, Rabelais, De la Boetie, Brantôme, Montaigne — they are all unquestionably alive, even to the humblest of the nameless students in the school of Abelard on the hill of Ste. Geneviève. The exuberance of life that there is in M. Flameng's nature is sometimes almost a misfortune, by inducing him to give too much attention to subordinate personages. For example, in the great composition that has for its subject Richelieu laying the foundation-stone of the Sorbonne church, the foreground is occupied by large figures of masons and others on a scaffolding, whilst Richelieu and his suite are away in the middle distance. M. Flameng has a taste in the picturesque that it is difficult to approve. He is extremely fond of scaffoldings, poles, ladders, cords, and planks, things that in the reality are but temporary encumbrances—so why make them permanent in a picture? The grand staircase at the Sorbonne is a finished piece of classical architecture, where ladders and planks would be out of place. Why paint them on the wall? The pretty and interesting composition in the same series which represents *Printing at Paris* (1469), is injured, though to a less degree, by the long lever of the screw press, which cuts the picture horizontally in two. The same taste for rather awkward things recurs in other well-known pictures by the artist, but in some of them, such as the *Players at Bowls* (Naples) and *Le Jeu de Fusil* (Dieppe, 1795), it does little or no harm. M. Flameng's extraordinary power of giving vitality to his conceptions of the past has never been seen to greater advantage than in his picture of *The French Army marching on Amsterdam* (1796). The ragged soldiery are making their

F. Flameng pinx.   François-Flameng—

The Chessplayers.

way painfully but bravely through the snow; never was army at once so miserable and so picturesque.

I may add that in addition to the most minute knowledge of costume, M. François Flameng is very accurate in his representation of buildings of very different styles, from the mediaeval fortifications of an old French town to the details of garden architecture in the eighteenth century. Besides this he is a good landscape-painter, and has mastered several different effects of light so as to paint them well from memory. For example, there is a fine effect when you look to the *east* and it is lighted by the flush of sunset. This effect has been painted more than once by M. Flameng, and with admirable truth, especially in his picture of *Rollin, principal du Collège de Beauvais, à Paris.*

An excellent example of what I have called ' historical *genre* ' is a picture by M. Toudouze, in the Salon of 1887, entitled *The Edict* (1626). The subject is Richelieu's stern edict against

THE EDICT (1626). *A FRAGMENT, BY E. TOUDOUZE.*

duelling, by which every surviving duellist incurred the penalty of death. In the picture, the edict itself is posted on a wall, but has been torn by a rebellious hand; the slain duellist is lying on the ground, and a monkish procession is issuing from the church, whilst soldiers are coming up the narrow street. The other duellist has disappeared. We should not call this an historical picture, as it does not represent any historical event, nor give the portrait of any known personage, and yet it is more than a simple *tableau de genre*, being connected with one of the most interesting things in history—the vain attempt of a wise ruler to put a stop to an insane practice, too profoundly rooted in the habits of his countrymen. The picture afforded, too, an opportunity for the contrast between life and death which has had an attraction for so many painters, especially French painters. There is the duellist himself, an hour ago ' in lusty life,' now motionless, and there is the contrast between his dreadful calm and the agitation of the living who come upon the scene.

There is a kind of historical *genre* which, without representing any particular incident, and without including the portrait of a single known personage, has for its object simply the realisation of a past time. An artist may propose to himself some date and place, and try to realise in his own mind the life of the nameless and forgotten common people, with the help of all that he knows about them and all that he can ascertain. The work is consequently *genre*, as it is not precisely either historical painting or landscape, yet there is a strong historical element in it, as it realises the past and helps the student of history to imagine life in another century with a probable approach to truth—a much nearer approach than would be possible for him without the help of pictorial art. In this way the book illustrations of M. Maurice Leloir, though drawn in our own time, are quite as good documents to help us to the understanding of life in the eighteenth century as the drawings and engravings that were executed in that century itself. Many other French artists, more or less known to fame, have devoted themselves to the study of the same epoch, and with the same intention of absolutely presenting it to us as it was. A picture by M. Bligny, in the Salon of 1890, may be taken as an example of a class. The artist proposed to himself as a subject, *A Décadi in Floréal*. The reader will remember that the *décadi* was the tenth day of the week of ten days in the Republican calendar, and *Floréal* was the month of April. The *décadi* was the day of rest answering to our Sunday, or, more accurately, to a French *dimanche*. So these soldiers of the revolutionary army are idling and talking, or going a-fishing, for there are

A DÉCADI IN FLORÉAL. BY A. BLIGNY.

hours of idleness and peace for individuals in the most disturbed times. Nothing can trouble the serenity of a French angler. During the last desperate conflict under the Commune, the anglers sat watching their floats bobbing in the ripples of the Seine.

M. Wagrez, though a Parisian by birth, and a pupil of Pils and Lehmann, has, during the last few years, attracted attention chiefly by pictures of Venetian and Florentine life in the fifteenth century. The interest of his pictures is chiefly external; I mean that it belongs to costume and architecture rather than to human character. The personages are well-made, richly dressed, and handsome; they group themselves in a stately manner, with magnificent architecture for a background. These pictures recall and realise for us a kind of existence which must have been more delightful for the eyes than that of any country or time since the fall of the Roman Empire. M. Wagrez paints all he has to paint with consummate skill, doing all his work most faithfully, down to every detail of ornament in architectural and other objects, and his figures are well grouped and behave in a properly genteel manner, as such very well-dressed people ought to do; but notwithstanding all these qualities and veracities, M. Wagrez does not make the past live again for us, simply because his personages are wanting in character. They are very excellent illustrations of fifteenth-century fashions.

Historical *genre* may be taken also to include what are commonly called 'incident pictures,' when the incident is taken from history. For example, suppose an elaborately painted interior of a drawing-room in the style of Louis XV. By itself such a subject would make a picture, and would be valued for its accuracy as a representation of architecture. If figures were introduced the same scene would become a *tableau de genre*, and if the figures were historical it would approach to the character of an historical painting, without, however, being called by that title unless the figures were made of supreme importance. In the Salon of 1888 M. Girardet had a picture entitled simply, *La Duchesse du Maine*, which, whilst truly historical, retained all the qualities and interest of a *tableau de genre*. The Duke of Maine was one of the Council of Regency under the Duke of Orleans, during the minority of Louis XV., and took part in a conspiracy against the Regent. As the Duchess had been active in the matter, both she and her husband were arrested on the 29th of December, 1718. The arrest of the lady in

her drawing-room is the subject of M. Girardet's picture, which was one of the most interesting of its class, avoiding the stiffness and formality of *la peinture d'histoire* as it used to be understood in France, and also the frivolity of the ordinary *genre* picture.

As I have mentioned in the earlier part of this chapter the mural paintings by M. François Flameng in the grand staircase of the Sorbonne, I may complete the notice of that decorative work by a short account of the pictures by M. Chartran. The upper floor of the staircase is divided into two large halls ; that to the right (as you enter) is filled with pictures by M. Flameng, and that to the left with an equal number of works by M. Chartran, an artist who may not have the brilliant gifts of his rival, but who has a strong and clear conception of the scenes that he undertakes to represent. His business appears to have been to illustrate the history of French science as M. Flameng illustrated that of literature. One of M. Chartran's principal compositions represents Ambroise Paré at the siege of Metz in 1553, when he first applied a ligature to an artery after the amputation of a limb, an improvement in surgery that spared mankind an infinity of suffering and an incalculable loss of life.* The artist has had the good taste to place the patient so that we do not see the limb, whereas we see the surgeon perfectly. The expression

A BAPTISM AT ST. MARK'S IN THE FIFTEENTH CENTURY. BY J. WAGREZ.

of grave self-possession on Paré's face, and of suffering endured with fortitude in that of the patient, as well as in his outstretched arm and clenched hand, is all that can be desired in a work of this character. Some wounded men and other onlookers are interested, without, perhaps, fully understanding the future importance of the experiment. A bishop is giving his benediction, and soldiers in the distance are running to defend the battlements. It would have been difficult to select a more interesting subject, and difficult to illustrate it better.

Another very admirable work in the same series has for its title *Louis IX. at the Abbey of Royaumont studies Mathematics under the direction of Vincent de Beauvais* (1223). This picture is charming for the dignity of the teacher and the earnest attentiveness of the royal pupil, as well as for the severe and simple taste with which the architecture and plain furniture are treated. It is unfortunate, but undeniable, that even the ability of an artist like M. Chartran is baffled by such a difficulty as that of costume. Surely, one may think, the intelligent expression of the faces, when the personages are the most intellectual men

---

* If I remember rightly, the practice of surgeons before the introduction of the ligature was to plunge the bleeding stump into boiling pitch, a process not only fearfully cruel but in most cases ineffective. The improvement introduced by Ambroise Paré was not only more humane, but at the same time a great advance in surgical efficiency.

M

in a great nation like France, ought of itself to predominate over such miserable details as those of tailoring. Well, no doubt it does so in real life, and also in literature, but not in pictorial art. Good costumes are a great help to the work of the painter, and bad costumes are an obstacle and an evil against which genius itself could never successfully contend. The power of costume has never been more strikingly exhibited than in M. Chartran's mural paintings at the Sorbonne. When he has to deal with Vincent de Beauvais and Louis IX. everything is in favour of dignity and nobleness ; when he comes to Ambroise Paré, to Descartes, or to Bernard Palissy lecturing on mineralogy, the costumes,

THE DUCHESS OF MAINE. BY J. GIRARDET.

if not severe, are at least picturesque and do no harm ; but when, after that, the artist tries to illustrate the career of Arago in the same way, exhibiting him as he lectured on astronomy, or when he shows Cuvier getting materials for his work on fossils, the result is perfectly disastrous. There are terrible portraits, too, of M. Renan and other contemporaries. I know that it is difficult to exclude the nineteenth century from scientific history, but it is a misfortune to have to paint it. Modern evening dress, for men, offers bad forms, a uniform dull texture, and no colour. Painters of contemporary French history have already been bold enough to undertake such subjects as presidential ceremonies with the Chief of the State in a black tail-coat. The President himself does escape from being absolutely uninteresting by the broad red ribbon of the Legion of Honour, but he dares not venture to wear the gold collar, as being too splendid for his simple dress. As for the ministers, they have nothing whatever to distinguish them, and the only relief is in the presence of military officers or ladies.

VII

The Rustic School

THE earliest predecessor of the present French rustic school was Léopold Robert, but he was unfortunate, both in his education and afterwards in the direction he took with regard to the study of nature. To understand Léopold Robert well is to appreciate the change that has come over French painting during the present century. It is never a waste of time to study a precursor: he helps us to know better that which we believed ourselves to know completely. Robert was born in 1794, near Neuchâtel, and he died at Venice in 1835. His art education began in 1810, and was entirely Parisian. It included both engraving and painting. As an engraver he won a 'second grand prix;' as a painter he worked hard under David, and afterwards established himself in Rome. The picturesque costumes of the Italian peasants first attracted him to rural life, but the effects of his early education, first as an engraver in a rigid style of burin engraving (etching was not understood or tolerated in those days), and afterwards as a painter in a very severe classical school, disqualified the artist for attaining a style in harmony with the picturesque subjects that he desired to paint. After attaining splendid success (he would not be a successful painter with such a style in the present day) he had the mortification of seeing his art go out of fashion, and after a hard struggle against technical difficulties, which have since been easily overcome by far inferior men, he put an end to his troubles by self-slaughter. Nevertheless, his reputation is not dead even at the present day. He is still popular in engravings, the copyists do not neglect his pictures, and the town of Neuchâtel has given a handsome price for one of them. But amongst painters it requires courage to mention him. Jules Breton, in his autobiography, says: 'So much the worse if I pass for a *bourgeois*, for a Philistine; I dismiss all false shame, and confess that I mean to speak of that poor Léopold Robert.'

He lived in a day when people cared more for art than for nature, so that there is much art in his works of a very obvious kind and less nature than in the present day, especially as to air, light and effect, and textures of all kinds. Nevertheless, Jules Breton says that Robert was not without some perception of the qualities he could not render, and that even his painting, such as it is, reveals this perception. The mental trouble that ended in suicide may have been due to the conflict between vague anticipations of the art of the future and technical inability to realise them.

Where Robert failed, Troyon brilliantly succeeded, and his success was due in great part to the absence of early education. Instead of the discipline of an engraver's desk or a painter's *atelier*, Troyon had nothing to help him but the fields and woods near Paris, and a little friendly advice. He came, too, under the influence of a really modern landscape-painter, Jules Dupré—an influence entirely wanting to Léopold Robert. In this manner, without being remote from art, as if he had lived far from the capital, Troyon was only helped by it instead of being overwhelmed, and he saw both landscape and animals with a freshness of eye quite modern. His success in a kind of art which is in reality composite was due to his possession of both its elements. The rustic painter is not simply a cattle-painter, or a successful student of the figure ; he must be a landscape-painter as well. He cannot depend upon figure-study in the *ateliers*, and yet it is necessary that he should have some knowledge of the figure, if only as an introduction to the study of organic form in animals.

The art of the rustic painter being composite, as it deals with animal form and landscape (seen together and under the same effects), it is likely to be in some respects inferior to each of the arts, taken separately, of which it is composed.

The intellectual rank of this department of art is inferior to its artistic rank. It has not the intellectual rank of the figure art that deals with the refinements of high culture or the depths of dramatic passion. On the other hand, if we look to the landscape side of it,

WEED BURNERS. BY L. E. ADAN.

rustic painting does not include much of the sublimity of landscape. As the figures of rustic painting are almost invariably uneducated peasants, so its landscape is usually common-place. Even when the sublimest landscape is close at hand, the rustic painter will turn away from it to seek for that simplicity which is most favourable to his own craft. In the Salon of 1886 there was a picture by F. Vuagnat, entitled *Shore of Lake Leman*. The title immediately conjures up before the mind's eye something very different from the shore of a common pond, yet M. Vuagnat had succeeded in finding the utmost commonplace even at Geneva, and painted nothing but a low bank with a bit of flat land, a roof amongst trees, some willows, and two white cows and a dark one. In the same Salon was a picture by M. Bonnefoy, called *The Close of a Fine Day*, and representing a most dreary landscape, without either wood or water, like one of the least interesting pieces of rising ground on an English moor. By itself such landscape could attract nobody, but in a picture it had the negative recommendation of not setting up a conflict with the cattle. It is for the same reason that in these rustic pictures the human beings are usually kept uninteresting and subordinate. They are so almost invariably in the works of Troyon and Rosa Bonheur. In Millet the case is different. He kept his landscape extremely simple, and significant only as a field for toil. It is sometimes dreary in the extreme, and bare of every kind of interest but that of human taskwork. Millet's animals are beautifully grouped, but have hardly any other interest or charm. He subordinated everything to his figures, and the figures themselves, by the law which seems to predominate over all rustic painting whatever, are almost mindless.

Both the human and the landscape interests in rustic art are therefore of an inferior kind. The best quality of it is a kind of poetry which in the best works pervades the whole subject. The French mind is generally favourable to this kind of poetry; it is not favourable to the grandest landscape. If all Frenchmen could read English, few would

appreciate Mr. Ruskin's chapters on 'Mountain Gloom' and 'Mountain Glory,' but thousands of Frenchmen are in perfect sympathy with the landscape sentiment of Virgil. There was in the seventeenth and eighteenth centuries, as we all know, a false pastoral sentiment in France. At a time when peasant life itself was completely wretched, being much worse than simply prosaic, the fine gentlefolks amused themselves by playing at a sort of game that represented an elegant rusticity. It was the quest of an ideal, though the ideal was vain and foolish. There was, however, so much of a right instinct in elegant pastoral sentiment, that rural life requires to be idealised if any great poetry or painting is to be made out of it at all.

The greatest danger of the present French school is a vulgar realism. Troyon was a very vigorous painter, with a strong grasp of reality; but the poetical element in

THE LAUNDRESS. BY JULES BRETON.

his art always preserved it from this evil. Rosa Bonheur has been saved from it by her excellent sense and taste. As for Millet, who composed generally with extreme care and who infused poetical or sympathetic sentiment into even the slightest of his works, he had no need to seek inspiration from Virgil, being his own poet. Millet was a poet who observed reality, and an artist who did not forget art in the presence of nature. The immortal element of his works is not the observation of peasant and animal life, it is the poetic sentiment. So, amongst the prosaic painting so common in the present day, any work of Jules Breton is sure to arrest attention by that quality or power, so difficult to define, which elevates art above reality, whilst preserving the clearest evidence of the closest study of reality. The embellishment of nature may come either from poetic sentiment or the special sense and culture of a painter—it does not come from a peasant's familiarity with nature. On this point the evidence of M. André Theuriet, the novelist, is conclusive. He says that the peasants themselves do not at all realise the charm that their life and its surroundings have for us; their work is too hard, and they are too much pinched between the two nippers of time and money, as the seasons never wait, neither does the landlord. The poetry of rustic life is in the mind of some educated spectator who has read Virgil or can appreciate painting. Millet is sometimes called a peasant painter because he lived very plainly and in the country. All that he had in common with prevalent French rustic sentiment was his compassion. The peasants have a feeling of compassion, not for people in other classes but for themselves. They *pity themselves* in their songs. Here is a short extract from a long, dreary *chanson bressane* quoted by M. Theuriet :—

> ' Le pauvre laboureur
> Il a bien du malheur ;
> Le jour de sa naissance,
> L'est déjà malheureux.

> ' Qu'il pleuve, tonne, ou grêle,
> Qu'il fasse mauvais temps,
> L'on voit toujours, sans cesse,
> Le laboureur aux champs.

> ' Le pauvre laboureur
> A de petits enfants ;
> Les met à la charrue
> A l'àge de quinze ans,
> Leur achète des guêtres ,
> C'est l'état du métier,
> Pour empêcher la terre
> D'entrer dans leurs souliers.'

And so the rustic song-maker goes on, sadly and wearily enumerating the toils of rural life without any Virgilian feeling for its charm. One of the very few pictures that represent peasant feeling accurately was entitled *His Own Land*, and represented a peasant digging vigorously an ugly and unpromising field in windy weather. Theuriet finds two happy times in this dreary peasant life. One is childhood, the country child being incomparably freer and happier than the town child, and especially happier than the poor little Parisian, cooped up in a tiny apartment on the top of a high house. The country child had a few years of blissful existence, light work and much play, with much enjoyment of nature—not aesthetic, but after his own fashion. This has lately been interfered with by compulsory education and long marches to school. The other happy time was the brief period before marriage and its cares, when the glamour of the sexual feeling gave an enchantment even to the hardest life. Theuriet notices the dread of old age in the peasant class, and the comparative indifference to death. Old folks feel themselves to be useless, and their children look upon them as a burden ; both consider the death of the aged as a deliverance, and there seems to be hardly anything of that tender sorrow for them that is common in more sensitive classes of society.

On all these points my own observation fully confirms that of Theuriet, and he agrees with me in the belief that all this genuine peasant life, that has inspired some of the best French artists of the present century, is destined shortly to disappear, when their works will gain a new and pathetic interest as the record of a vanished past. Even already the rising generation, the young men of twenty, have neither the old simplicity of life and thought nor the old attachment to the soil. Education and railways are the two persistent agents that produce the mental change, and besides this there is a material and economical change in the introduction of scientific agriculture. The pastoral and agricultural life commemorated by Millet, Troyon, and Rosa Bonheur was still essentially primitive, and there lay half its poetic and artistic charm. Consider such things as a plough, a cart, a waggon drawn by oxen—all made in the village or at the farm itself, never painted, and taking with time grey colouring and rough texture from sun and rain, in beautiful harmony with the land :

JULIEN DUPRE 1885

Julien Dupré pinx.

Imp. Chardon-Wittmann. Paris.

H. Toussaint sculp.

THE HAYFIELD

compare with these implements some iron machine, very hard in outline and painted red or blue! There was a picture by M. Lorieux in the Salon of 1890 representing a new-fangled iron plough, very neat, and drawn with the same careful accuracy that a Parisian painter of street scenes will put into a perambulator; but what could Millet have done with such a plough? I notice, too, that a few of the younger painters, who think it right to paint whatever they see, are introducing the steam-engine into their agricultural pictures. The old farm buildings, with their picturesque thatch and their interesting irregularities, have been replaced in many instances, and will be ultimately in all, by strictly rectangular edifices with slate roofs.

Émile van Marcke, who died at the close of 1890, was, artistically speaking, the son of Troyon, and, like him, worked at one time in the porcelain manufactory at Sèvres. He was not exactly a pupil of Troyon in the ordinary sense, but worked under his personal influence. Van Marcke had not the poetical gift of his predecessor, and was more strictly what we usually understand by the term 'cattle-painter.' He was an admirable artist within his own limits, and he exercised a healthy

THE YOUNG OXEN. BY E. B. DEBAT-PONSAN.

influence on the French school. Throughout his career he set an excellent example of patient industry in study. During the summer he painted studies of animals from nature, out of doors each of them costing fifteen or twenty sittings, and he never would part with one of them. His pictures were not studies, but carefully thought-out compositions, however apparently simple in subject. Instead of becoming negligent as his wealth increased, he employed his leisure in learning more.* His art was as sober as it was learned and free from eccentricity. In one respect it may be regretted that his example is not more generally followed in the contemporary school. He knew the difference between a study and a picture,† as Jules Breton afterwards defined it in these words :—

'What we call a study is a fragment, a note, a piece of information, and cannot constitute a *whole*. Objects are taken for themselves, and no correlation makes them take a share in the expression of some general idea. A picture, on the contrary, ought to be a concert of elements, uniting together for a common purpose.'

In the younger French school, the dislike to obviously artificial arrangements (and

---

* See the very interesting account of Van Marcke by M. Emile Michel, published in 'L'Art,' April 15th, 1891.

† The painting of *Draught Horses*, by G. Hélie, modestly called 'a study' by its author, is in fact more of a picture than many modern works that claim the more ambitious title.

almost any arrangement is obvious to an artist) has caused in many instances the substitution of the study for the picture.

This is never the case in the works of Jules Breton himself. Whatever he exhibits is sure to be a picture, and likely, at the same time, to be a poem. But Jules Breton is already an old man, and, though working vigorously still, does not belong to the present generation, which produces more students than artists. Such pictures as *The Last Ray* (1885), a scene of rural life in the evening, are uncommon in the new school, not for want of materials or lack of knowledge, but from the rarity of inspiration. A peasant and his wife are returning home after sunset ; a little child runs to greet them, and the old folks are sitting out of doors, by the grandmother's spinning-wheel. There you have the idyllic aspect of rural life, with pictorial unity and truth at the same time, but not the prosaic truth. Even the single figures by Jules Breton have always some special dignity or interest. *The Song of the Lark* (1885) represents a peasant-girl pausing as she listens to the lark ; *The Shepherd's Star* has for its heroine a strong peasant-woman carrying home a sack on her head, with a severe, almost tragical expression ; and *The Laundress* is a variation of the same subject, the burden in this case being a basket of clothes. The painter agrees with the one humane saying of Napoleon, ' Respect the burden, Madam ! '

DRAUGHT HORSES. A STUDY. BY G. HELIE.

M. Jules Didier has for many years been one of the leading French cattle-painters, and he still keeps well to the front. I should describe him rather as a landscape and cattle painter than as a rustic painter, in the sense of being profoundly impressed by that poetry of rural life which was the motive of Millet and Breton. Suppose an artist who understands all the elements of landscape, who can paint skies well, and trees, and everything from the transient effect on distant hills to the elaborated detail of a foreground. To this knowledge and accomplishment add a thorough knowledge of animal form both in rest (as in the picture of cattle in the Roman Campagna) and in action (as in *The Wheat Waggon*, or *The Two Bulls and the Frog*), and you have an artist well equipped for work in the fields, and likely to be able to deal with anything he will find there. Nor can it be said that M. Didier's work is ever marred by defects of taste. There is nothing in common between him and the vulgar realists ; but, on the other hand, there is no striking revelation of anything hitherto undiscovered, so that the artist has only a place in the second rank, though that place is an honourable one. A work outside of his usual simple naturalism was a frieze illustrating field labours, designed on decorative principles for the City of Paris, and giving a *résumé* of the artist's knowledge in a form severely conventionalised.

M. Julien Dupré (who, when the initial only is given, may sometimes be confounded with the landscape-painter, Jules Dupré) is not only an observant cattle-painter, but a very forcible artist. Few contemporary painters equal him in vivid and powerful realisation. His subjects are the simple old subjects : cows drinking from a tub that a woman is filling or from a tub already full, with a woman looking on and a sheep browsing beside her—or else

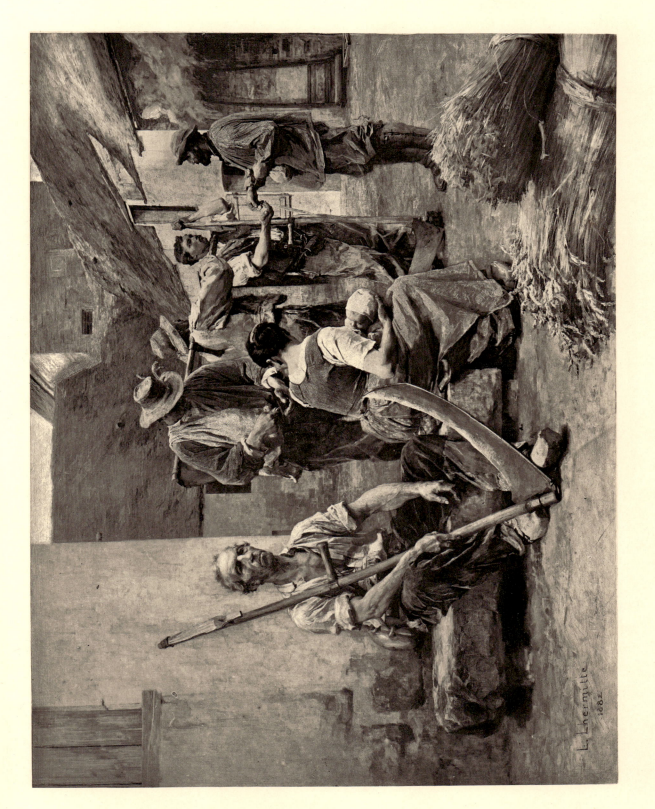

Pay time in Harvest.

it may be milking-time and the women come with their pails—or perhaps a cow has taken that imaginary powder which the French call *la poudre d'escampette*, and is running she knows not whither, not yet arrested by the farmer's lad who scampers by her side. The subjects, as we see, are commonplace enough, they are not intellectually or spiritually very deep, but when we approach them from the artistic side they may assume another aspect. For example, *The White Cow*, in the Salon of 1890, was a brilliantly successful study of white in full sunshine and of its values when lighted only by reflection. At the same time, in the background, the painter had a delightfully quiet space of shaded wall, giving sufficient strength of opposition to the animal without blackness, chiaroscuro far superior both in science and art to that of the old masters who are most praised for their chiaroscuro. Another admirable quality in M. Julien Dupré is his quietly truthful observation of character, both human and animal, and his unfailing good taste in the arrangement of simple materials.

Nothing can be more agreeable to a critic than complete knowledge, in a painter, of the resources of art along with moderation in the use of them. This painter always makes the best of his materials by judicious concentration and opposition, without insisting too much. There is seldom any novelty in his subject (the interest taken by some peasants in a passing balloon being a rare exception), and he does not seek for novelty in eccentricity.

Artists eminent in other ways have sometimes painted rustic pictures from a love of the

A WAGGON OF WHEAT. BY JULES DIDIER.

country and its occupations. M. Dagnan-Bouveret, whose interest in the serious and religious aspects of rural life has led him to paint works that are now celebrated, has occasionally illustrated its more trivial incidents when men and animals are associated together. He is always a most careful and truthful painter, whatever he has to deal with, but his style is hardly picturesque enough to enable him to make the most of animals. The most famous animal-painters have succeeded rather by the animation they throw into their creatures, and by the attractions of colour and texture, than by perfection of line.

On the human side, no French artist of the present day has succeeded more completely in the representation of rural life than M. Lhermitte. His knowledge of the peasantry is of that intimate kind that only comes from constant observation. He lives a great part of the year in a picturesque village near the Marne: 'One of those corners of French ground,' says Theuriet, 'which contain in a narrow space a great variety of culture and landscape.' Here he finds all that he needs for his rustic art, both in fields and vineyards and in the houses. *Pay-time in Harvest* is one of the most notable of his rustic pictures, but there are so many others that a book of engravings from them would already form an epitome of peasant life. In such a book it is likely that the restful subjects would predominate over the laborious ones. M. Lhermitte is too much of an artist not to perceive that repose is better adapted than action to the purposes of art, and the repose he paints is the best of all, that which comes after the hardest work in the burning sun of harvest. In the *Reapers' Rest* (1890), a man is sitting wearily on the ground whilst a woman

o

holds a *cruche* for a kneeling girl to drink from.   In the picture of *Thirst* (1890) it is the man who drinks, like a traveller in the desert.   In *Rest* (1888) a baby is drinking its mother's milk, the father tenderly looking on.   In *Wine*, a robust workman is refreshing himself with a glass as he takes a brief interval of idleness.   In the picture of *Hay-time*, the man who works hardest is seated on the ground and sharpening his scythe with a hammer on his little portable anvil—a picture so true that only the tinkling sound of the hammer-strokes is necessary to complete the illusion.

It may be observed, with regard to all these pictures of rustic life, that vineyards and the labours connected with wine are much less frequently illustrated than the meadow and the cornfield.   The reason, probably, is to be found in the unpicturesque character of the French vineyards themselves, which are not inviting to an artist except for a short time during the change of colour in autumn.   The forests are more interesting, and the wood-cutter's life in them has been in some degree illustrated by Dameron and others ; we remember, too, the picture of *The Charcoal Burners*, by Rosa Bonheur, which was a faithful representation of human labour, though painted chiefly for the oxen.   Still, the interior of the great French forests does not much attract landscape-painters on account of the want of distances ('you cannot see the forest for the trees'), and the service of animals is confined to carting, whilst it is much more varied on the farms.

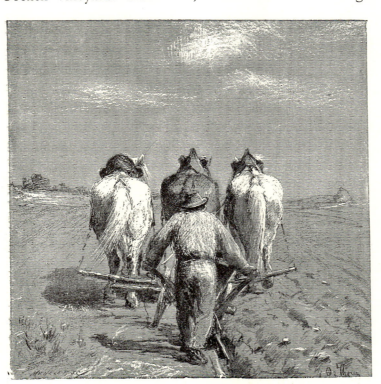

IN AUTUMN.   BY O. DE THOREN.

I have not space at the close of this chapter to do more than mention a few of the more distinguished younger rustic painters.   M. De Thoren died before the opening of the Salon in the Champ-de-Mars in 1890, after contributing nine pictures.   The picture by M. Debat-Ponsan, of which we give a sketch, was exhibited in 1891.   That by M. Adan, *Brûleuses d'Herbes*, was exhibited the year before.   Both these artists have a sense of grace in attitude and in the composition of their subjects that elevates their work above what Theuriet calls 'le parti-pris brutal et faux de l'école dite *naturaliste*.'

VIII

Some Caricaturists

FRANCE is more old-fashioned than England in her ideas about caricature. In England the genuine old caricature is almost extinct, and in place of it we have sketching with accent and more or less exaggeration, but little of that wild boyish delight in making people hideous that cheered the life of our grandfathers. Mr. George du Maurier takes too much pleasure in his own observant veracity to be a real caricaturist. Mr. Tenniel is a thoughtful and severe satirist, living intellectually above the ordinary level of caricature, and only adopting one or two of its methods, such as the intentional deterioration of bodily forms. Charles Keene was an unsurpassed student of character in the middle and lower classes, but too truthful for caricature of the old kind. Mr. Furniss is a genuine caricaturist, who has revived old-fashioned extravagance in a modern form, but who does not make a mechanical habit of it, as he turns at will to character-sketching, with no more exaggeration than is necessary to make commonplace personages amusing. In France, on the contrary, the systematically extravagant caricature is still a regular article of commerce. There is the 'Grelot,' for example, a journal never seen in private houses, but which has a large circulation in *cafés*. We have nothing in England like the 'Grelot.' It might have succeeded in the eighteenth century, unless the Government had suppressed it for attacking Ministers, but our taste in the nineteenth would have left it without sale. Every week the 'Grelot' gives a large coloured caricature, usually on some social or political subject of the day. These caricatures are now numerous enough to fill an extensive gallery, and a strange collection it would be! It would reflect the coarse cleverness, the cruel, pitiless ill-nature, the dirtiness, the self-conceit, and the rabid hatred of foreigners that characterise the vulgar French mind. The technical qualities of these caricatures are always uniformly the same. The drawing is clear, hard, and in its way accomplished, but without taste or amenity. It harmonises perfectly with the merciless decision of the attacks on men or nations. Additional distinctness is given by the colouring, like that of a map, in crude greens, reds, and yellows, with a flesh-tint according to rule. All faces are made hideous in proportion to the hatred excited by their owners, and yet, in the case of public men, with an undeniable and (to the victims) a painful preservation of a likeness. In political caricatures of this class the very worst and lowest motives are always attributed. There is seldom anything of what we call humour, and the wit that there is springs entirely from malevolence; it is never tender or kindly.

If all French caricatures were of the kind that I have just attempted to describe, the study of them would offer very little interest or variety. The English reader cares very little for ferocious attacks on French politicians, and still less for onslaughts on Germans, Italians, and his own countrymen, which proceed in most cases from ignorance and from an intolerance of the foreigner common to the vulgar of all nations. Happily, however, there is a large field of modern French caricature that repays the student, and although if taken in the mass it is too much infected with silliness and impurity to be acceptable without choice, it would be possible to cull from it a rich collection full of the most various human interest.

Without forgetting the clever men of former times, such as Gavarni and 'Cham'—who, like all men of original genius, can never be replaced — it may, I think, be reasonably maintained that French caricature has made progress during the last twenty years. The best of it is much more refined and artistic than it used to be, it is in far better taste. The cleverest men unite in their work the sense of the ridiculous with a love of elegance in costume and form and of grace in attitude. They also evidently like to make their work decorative, and they try, when possible, to cater for the pleasure of the eye. These tendencies are quite opposed to the old habits of the caricaturist, who cared for nothing but the fullest expression of his ill-nature. An excellent example of this modern tendency to beauty in caricature, or at least in humorous sketching, is the work of 'Mars,' already well known in England by his contributions to the 'Graphic.' Convinced that a pretty face is more agreeable to look upon than an ugly one, and that effective patterns in dresses are more interesting than those which are insignificant, 'Mars' seldom fails to make his sketches at once pretty and amusing. From the technical point of view, both 'Mars' and several other men are distinguished by a clearness in design and a vigour of opposition unknown to the earlier caricaturists, and these qualities are due to the modern understanding of limitations in pen-drawing, which cannot deal with infinite gradations of shade, but is effective with the simpler elements of white and black and two greys, accompanied by clear linear definition. Every artist has his favourite types of character. 'Mars' likes to draw young ladies who are pretty and fashionable, and who display, not impudence, but a prodigious degree of tranquil self-possession. His children are active, healthy, and full of play. He treats both women and children with a certain gentlemanly tenderness, and is not blind to their beauty or their charm. His treatment of the adult male Frenchman is not so gentle, and curiously insists upon those peculiarities and defects which strike the eye of an Englishman, so that his satire seems almost English satire directed against our neighbours. The worst objection to the abundant work of 'Mars' is that its treatment of feminine failings is too monotonous. The young women are almost invariably pretty, neatly dressed, and bold. I may add that the accessories are always well observed, and cleverly, if slightly, represented. This, too, is a modern characteristic, for the old caricaturist did not think it worth while to bestow serious attention on furniture and equipage. Again, although 'Mars' is alive to the faults of a society that hardly even pretends to be virtuous, he is never coarse.

Caricaturists appear to be fond of pseudonyms. The artist who calls himself 'Caran d'Ache' (pronounced 'd'Ash') is of all living caricaturists the most original and inventive. He has carried *narrative* caricature to a degree of perfection unknown before his time. No one ever rivalled him in that kind of imagination which perceives beforehand how an absurd situation may be prepared for so as to become inevitable. Sketch after sketch leads you gradually up to it, and if you guess what is coming you see that there is no escape. As linear drawing, often of extreme simplicity, and at other times with a more elaborate decorative intention, the work of Caran d'Ache is of first-rate artistic excellence. When his intention is simply to tell a little story laconically, he remembers that brevity is the soul of wit and reduces the number of his lines to the fewest possible. When he is in the humour for the grotesque, as for example in the uniform of some pompous court, his work becomes ornate, elaborate, and at the same time effectively decorative. It is always, however, firmly and decidedly linear. It is connected, technically, with the earliest forms of line-engraving and with primitive Asiatic design. We ought to be very careful about the application of the epithet 'great' to artists and their works. We live in an age when there is 'little that's great, but much of what is clever,' but I should say that Caran d'Ache is really a great artist, both by the strength and fecundity of his invention, by his wit and humour, and by his rare technical qualities.

M. Robida was known before Caran d'Ache, and has long enjoyed a more popular if less artistic reputation. His subjects are usually found either in the extravagances of contemporary life and costume, or in fanciful anticipations of the future. He has travelled, too, and taken his sketch-book with him. It is long since he published a volume of clever sketches from Switzerland, and I remember some sketches of London, not omitting that fog which is so interesting and even agreeable to our neighbours. There was a sad accident in one of those foggy sketches; a hansom ran into an omnibus from behind, so that the horse got inside the omnibus. They always do so *à Londres*. M. Robida did ample justice to the more dismal aspects of the Thames; it was not his business, as a Gallic satirist, to expatiate upon its beauties. In the streets, he took note of many things peculiarly English —the policeman, the shoe-black, the gin-shop, &c., &c.—just as our own caricaturists are attracted by what is most French in Paris. Not that M. Robida is blinded by his patriotism to what is ridiculous in Parisian life itself. He delights in the extravagances of costume, and being gifted with a strong instinct for decorative exuberance, he makes the utmost of every suggestion afforded by the caprice of fashion. It is amusing to observe the persistence of this decorative instinct. In one of M. Robida's sketches illustrating 'Les Grands Jours de la Vie,' a little black dog is made to come in as part of the decoration along with the blacks in the ladies' dresses. The dresses themselves are always *consistently* exaggerated: I mean, that the artistic sense and significance of the design are first accepted, and then the exaggeration is no more than a carrying out of the same principle to possible, if extreme, consequences. Here is a costume for the varnishing day at the Salon of the Champ de Mars (fashion of 1890). The young lady thinks, 'I already wore this toilette at the varnishing day at the Champs Elysées; it is too simple. I ought to have worn something more for the varnishing at the Champ de Mars.'

COSTUME FOR A VARNISHING DAY.
BY A. ROBIDA.

M. Robida is humane enough to have some pity for the victims who visit picture-galleries in obedience to fashion. In a sketch of a wedding tour he shows the pair seated on a bench, utterly exhausted with 'six leagues of compulsory galleries' under the tyranny of 'the terrible Michelangelo, the ferocious Raphael, and those Primitives, dear madam!' It is rather unfortunate that we cannot give one of those coloured prints in which the variegated hues of the dresses add so much to the spectator's pleasure or amazement. In black and white Robida is at his best in the pompous Parisian wedding.

Colour may sometimes add greatly to the force of ridicule in a caricature. In one of 'Job's' caricatures, a lady, travelling towards Paris, displays a green-backed volume with red edges. Her husband exclaims, 'What an idea, to buy such a book!' so the lady answers that it harmonises with her dress, which is also green and red. Is not that a satisfactory reason for book-buying? The judicious use of colour in caricature may often heighten the absurdity of a figure. In a large coloured caricature by 'Job' some officers are inspecting recruits, and amongst the recruits is an *artiste dramatique* (what we call an actor), who is taking off his hat with much grace. The

P

THE WEDDING.   BY A. ROBIDA.

actor is certainly made more delightful by his yellow ochre suit and his pale blue cravate *à la Vallière.*

We may notice one peculiarity about French caricatures of military subjects : they are at the same time full of intimate knowledge of military habits and of kindly feeling. If they laugh at officers and soldiers, they do it in a friendly way. This is because the French army is now such a thoroughly national institution, and not a body of men, apart from civilians, that might be used for oppression. When, however, the French caricaturist undertakes to illustrate foreign armies we see at once that he lacks knowledge, and that his temper is no longer quietly humorous, but acid and hostile. He tries to make Italians, Germans, and Englishmen as ridiculous as he can. 'Drum,' the caricaturist, does not like the German and Italian alliance, and his harmless vengeance consists in making a German and an Italian officer physically inelegant. The Italians, as we learn from these caricatures, are enormously fat, the Germans egregiously tall. Englishmen are self-indulgent. An English sentry in one of the colonies wears a cool pith helmet and veil, and sits in an easy rocking-chair looking out to sea. On a table by his side is a glass with a bottle of soda-water, and a negro brushes away the flies. Even Her Majesty is not spared ; however, the caricature is not very offensive. She is represented as a German colonel of dragoons, going to inspect her regiment in full uniform and almost spherical in figure. The caricaturist who calls himself 'Pencil' deals cleverly with military subjects. He has much technical power as a pen-draughtsman. His soldiers and officers are strongly characterised, and sometimes he attacks civilians—as, for example, in four very humorous studies of lecturers, represented by *The Learned Lecturer, The Anarchical Lecturer, The German Lecturer on Philosophy,* and *The Amusing, Amiable Lecturer.*

'TU T'ES TROMPÉ, JOSEPH,' ETC. BY DRANER.

Much of the military business for the journal 'La Caricature' is done by Draner, who also deals with sportsmen and domestic servants in great houses. As a specimen of the last, here is a sketch of a footman's disappointment. He says to the cook, 'You made a mistake, Joseph ; you gave the good coffee to the monkeys (their masters), and now we shall have to content ourselves with rinsings in the servants' hall.' Sometimes Draner goes back to a past time—for example, to the days of Louis Philippe—and makes the most of the old fashions, so curious and ridiculous to us now.

Elderly readers may remember a time, before the invention of photography, when portraits used to be cut out in black paper and pasted on a white ground. The black silhouette survives in French caricature, and is practised with much skill by 'Sorel.' The attitudes of his little figures are often very clever and expressive. There is a mixed method by which the black silhouette is sometimes introduced into coloured caricatures ; but this, I think, is a mistake, because the black figures look like chimney-sweeps.

The best use of black is to fill spaces in linear drawing. The comic sketches of Albert Guillaume are technically excellent. His method of drawing is very clear and very simple, and his blacks have a great expressional value. For example, there is a subject of a schoolboy returning to school after his holidays. The schoolmaster is a big man with a white beard and a black costume. The solemn and pompous character of the pedagogue is greatly helped by all that printers' ink, and his beard looks the whiter for the contrast In 1890 M. Guillaume contributed to the 'Caricature' a set of sketches entitled *Ressemblance Funeste*, representing three old gentlemen, very much alike, who all inquire successively of a policeman where the Rue Jean Bart is.   He thinks they are all one man,

THE ARCHITECT'S VISIT. BY ALBERT GUILLAUME.

and is furious at the third. Technically, these sketches may be noticed for the clever employment of white, black, and a single grey. The three colours give much liveliness and distinctness to the drawings. Besides technical merits M. Guillaume has the invaluable talent of representing people as so entirely absorbed in their occupations that they entirely forget appearances. In *The Architect's Visit* ('Revue Illustrée') an architect is announced to a gentleman by his servant; he enters with a roll, opens it, spreads it on the floor, and they both finally get down on their knees upon the paper. So, in *Un Plan*, a thin architectural draughtsman becomes more and more absorbed in his work, and finally bends completely over his drawing-board. In *A Very Complicated Stroke* a billiard-player is represented alone, and our pleasure is to observe the odd attitudes of a fat gentleman intent upon his object and unconscious that he is watched.

M. Godefroy is technically as clever as M. Guillaume, but his invention of situations is not so original or so lively. Sometimes, however, the mere words, without the drawing, are amusing. A gentleman and his wife are seated by the fireside when she says, 'What a strange institution marriage is amongst the Mormons—four or five wives!' His reflection is, 'Very bad system; small hopes of becoming a widower!' Godefroy's absent man who asks for absinthe in a church is but a poor invention in comparison with Sorel's absinthe-drinker who plunges into the water up to his knees at the *Fontaines Lumineuses* and is called back by a policeman, when he answers: 'I cannot see absinthe flowing like that without tasting it!' The sight of the green water had been too much for him.

Godefroy's *Bonne Bouteille* is of slight importance as a subject, but the sketches are excellent. Two friends go together to *diner sur l'herbe*. They have a precious bottle of wine, too well corked. One after the other tugs at the cork; at last it yields. The gentleman in black sits down and drinks, the other goes to fetch water from a pump. *A Mother-in-Law's Dream* represents a middle-aged lady asleep on a shadeless bench in midsummer. She dreams that she melts away in water and becomes a rivulet. Delight of her son-in-law at the unhoped-for liquefaction!

THE GOOD BOTTLE. BY GODEFROY.

There is more invention in a series of six pictures by Radiguet. A girl is looking over a high garden-wall, and a young man approaches on horseback. He ties his horse and climbs a rope-ladder. He takes the lady's hand affectionately. Suddenly her father appears on the scene with a pistol, and offers Death or Marriage. The young gentleman prefers marriage, and signs a formal promise before a notary. The girl is presented to him in a

A MONK'S FUN

room, when he discovers that she is a *cul-de-jatte* (that she has no legs), a little deficiency that had been concealed by the garden-wall.

M. Le Mouel, unlike most Parisians, seems to be acquainted with the dull and monotonous existence of a little provincial town. He shows us the devout old women going to early mass; the idlers on the bridge (bridges are always a favourite resort of idlers); the doctor's ride through the little town, when he is stopped by people who want to consult him; and, finally, a sitting of the Town Council. The same artist once published a large coloured sketch entitled *Bourgeois*, in which a child and its grandfather are gathering mushrooms. 'Are these mushrooms poison, grandfather?' 'I really don't know, but we will send them as a present to cousins Lambert, and if they do them no harm we can eat the mushrooms ourselves.' In another sketch our author dines with a *bourgeois*, who says to him: 'I don't know much about your business, but I suppose it must be as it is in the cloth trade, the big houses kill the little ones.'

'Luque' has made many caricature portraits of celebrities on rather a large scale, increased still further by the old-fashioned practice of putting a big head on a small body. There is a sound reason for this in the economy of space. When natural proportions are observed the body occupies room disproportionate to the interest of it. In all those portraits by Luque of which I know the originals, the likeness has been cleverly preserved. Louise Michel (with eagle's body and wings), the Shah of Persia, M. Carnot after his election, Jules Verne, General Boulanger (as a king), Gérôme, the painter, and many others, are striking though not exactly flattering likenesses.

The best gift for contemporary caricature is not the highest gift. There is Vierge, for example, whose genius for the grotesque is almost too good for ordinary application, and seems to require the stately Spanish costumes of the sixteenth and seventeenth centuries. Vignola is, perhaps, better for our own time. He seems to have learned much from Robida, though without imitating his exaggerations. Vignola indicates much detail with his lines, such as the pattern of ladies' dresses, the stripes and plaids in male costumes, the reticulations of game-bags, &c., all which add truth of character, though at the expense of truth of effect.

*ASSIGNING THEATRICAL PARTS. BY
A. VIGNOLA.*

This account of French caricature has left many names unnoticed, especially amongst artists already well known before the most modern time began. There has certainly been a great technical improvement in modern work, but manual cleverness and technical intelligence have not always, or often, been seconded by wit and invention in the subjects. Modern caricaturists appear to be the opposite, or at least the converse, of 'Cham.' His drawings were all alike, the mechanical repetition of a lesson once learned, but his ideas were inexhaustible. The modern caricaturist is usually far superior as a draughtsman, but he seldom hits upon an idea that is really interesting or humorous in the verbal expression separately from the design.

An intermediate art between caricature and serious painting is that kind of humorous painting which exists only to amuse. It differs from caricature in avoiding the exaggeration of forms, and it differs from serious art in distracting the spectator's attention from beauty or accuracy of design to whatever levity there may be in the idea. The painter finds in this both a gain and a loss—a gain in the attention of a multitude without much care for art, and a loss in the facility with which his more purely artistic qualities may be overlooked. This is M. Jules Garnier's position. In such a picture as a *A Monk's Fun*, he amuses us

Q

with a sketch of character that might have suited a professed caricaturist, and yet he bestows upon it quite as much serious workmanship as if the subject itself were serious. For my part, I cannot see pictures of this class without a feeling of regret, as the laugh which it is their purpose to excite might have been caused equally by a slight sketch, whilst the patient and accomplished craft might have been bestowed on some subject that we should care to dwell upon. However, this is one of the forms of contemporary art, and one in which considerable mental ability is united to great technical skill.

IX

Portrait and Landscape

IT is the custom in France to give rarely the name of a private person whose portrait is exhibited in the Salon, a reticence which deprives many valuable works of that interest and individuality in the pages of the critic to which their merit might have entitled them. What can be more difficult than to remember a portrait by a letter of the alphabet? The majority are not indicated otherwise. We have Monsieur C. and Madame D. and in others the sexes may be different whilst the letters remain the same. Such is the importance of a name as a help to memory that almost all anonymous portraits fade from our recollection immediately, whilst those with names, if their merit is equal, have a chance of being remembered for some years. Painters might take a hint from the compilers of catalogues. A picture was called 'Portrait de Madame D.' and we forgot it; had it been called 'The Lady with one Glove' we might have remembered it. Some peculiarity in the title is a great help to memory. M. Pille exhi-

bited in 1887 a portrait of Vayson, the painter, and as Vayson was one of his friends he called the picture affectionately *L'ami Vayson*, which does much to fix it in our minds, as the title is rarely given. So it is when the rank or function of the sub-ject is in any way extraordinary. The fine portrait of M. Péladan by M. Desboutin (1891) ought to have been called the Sar Péladan, because 'Sar' is a very rare title belonging, I believe, to necromancy.

*PORTRAIT OF MÈRE STE. URSULE. BY
A. F. GORGUET.*

There are two qualities in portrait-painting that have to be reconciled before there can be any com-plete success. These are pictorial excellence and likeness. Except in the case of public men a critic has rarely an opportunity of judging likeness. He may praise unreservedly some beautiful picture that bears little or no resemblance to the original. There is, however, a certain temper of veracity, a desire to be truthful, which is usually recognisable in an artist's work, and certainly this temper has never been so common in French art as it is now. It is surprising how many artists have abandoned the old French notions of prettiness and elegance which led to so much flattery in portrait-painting, replacing them by the endeavour to interpret character of the most various kinds. Many French painters have exercised their talents in painting their relations. Sometimes the relations are gentlefolks, but their gentility is shown by simplicity and good taste rather than by any affectation; more frequently the artist's relations belong to the middle or lower classes, and there is no attempt to make them seem genteel. Democracy has had its influence in the painting of people who are not relations. In 1889 M. Rixens exhibited a portrait of a middle-class man at his ease, in every-day costume, legs crossed, hands in pockets, a lively expression on his face, no dignity but much life. There is a whole class of portraits that connect the subjects directly with their professional avocations. *L'ami Vayson*, by M. Pille, represented the artist in his studio, with its furniture and a dozen canvases about him. M. Rousseau, inspired by Rembrandt, painted the medical professor C. (how much more satisfactory it is to know that Rembrandt's professor was called Tulp!) with a corpse before him on the dissecting-table. M. Weerts painted M. Hugues, the sculptor, in his studio, and crushed (I speak metaphorically) by one of his own statues. But the most remarkable portraits of this class are those of scientific celebrities by Lhermitte, who makes them the centre of an attentive auditory.

PORTRAIT OF MADAME N. DE LA T. BY
J. V. VERDIER.

The fine arts do not pretend to be stately or dignified professions, so when M. Carrière paints M. X., the sculptor, he dresses him in the simple and easy *costume d'atelier* (trousers and a jersey), and makes him come forward naturally as if to receive a visitor, whilst he squeezes a little clay between his fingers. The stately professions are chiefly the magistracy and the Church, and these are often represented in robes and vestments, with all the insignia of rank. There are also the various quieter costumes of the religious orders, which are almost invariably good for pictorial purposes on account of their sobriety and dignity. An example is the portrait of *Mother Ursula, Superior of the Convent of St. Quay*, painted by M. Gorguet, and exhibited in the Salon of 1888. Democracy has hardly affected this class of subject. In 1891 M. Baschet paints a *Président de la Cour de Cassation*, in his ermine, with as much dignity as an English painter could give to a Lord Chancellor on the woolsack. The other sex has no need of magisterial rank to assume the dignity of robes. With the help of a stately dress and an arm-chair a private lady may look very much like a queen, as for example in M. Verdier's picture of *Madame N. de la T.* Another very queenly portrait is that of *Madame Benjamin Constant*, by her husband. She is dressed in black velvet, with long yellow gloves, and stands before a rich tapestried background. At her foot is a cushion with gold embroidery, a wonderful bit of painting. In a work of this serious kind it is evident that the painter has put forth his whole strength, and that he has been anxious to enrich it with all his great technical accomplishment, acquired in laborious years. No crude young talent could find the trick of such painting as that. When, however, we pass to the kind of portrait-painting which is most recent (for although Constant is still living he is not of the new school), we find a more perilous principle of work—more perilous because relying rather on a stroke of cleverness, or sudden inspiration, than upon learning and patient skill. There is M. Besnard, for example, who exhibited in 1891 a picture of two young ladies with a forest background. The girls are both lively and graceful, but the system of painting, especially of mingled greens and blues in the background, involves such complete reliance upon the good luck of the moment that it is either hit or miss. So it is with the astonishing portrait of *M. Renouard*, the draughtsman, by M. Mathey, which seizes upon a moment of intense attention, when the subject is hard at work, and looking at you as if he would look into your brain. Considered as a representation of life the picture is a complete success, but it is painted with a sort of masterly crudeness that is full of risk. Painters like M. Besnard and M. Mathey are not troubled with any of that timidity, or dread of doing wrong, which Mulready thought necessary to a student. No one could paint as they do without an immense self-confidence, but it has a double result in the liveliness of the portrait and the crudeness of the picture. The portraits by M. Carrière avoid crudity of colour by a voluntary restriction to a system that is almost monochrome, whilst as the artists just mentioned are full of life in their representations of humanity, so M. Carrière seems to prefer a dim limbo of sadness that lies halfway between life and death. If the newspapers had not told us that M. Daudet, the novelist, was unhappily in bad health, we should have known it from his portrait, which is that of a saddened invalid. The artist's remarkable power of expressing sadness is shown in another portrait, that of a woman, entitled *Rêverie*. His method of painting is very peculiar—it is marked by an abuse of blending with the softening tool; but the painter can be precise enough when he likes, and he draws in reality admirably whilst avoiding linear definition. In this respect M. Carrière is exactly the opposite of M. Saintin, and also in preferring extreme simplicity of subject and the fewest materials, whilst M. Saintin delights in the accumulation of objects. His portrait of Madame Carnot is crowded with costly furniture, wrought with the utmost elaboration. Amongst the painters who work with extreme industry and conscientiousness in the representation of persons and things, M. Friant now occupies a very distinguished place. His veracity, both in the repre-

sentation of human character and of objects, is equal to that of the masters who painted before brush-work had taken the place of delineation. The portraits of the two actors Coquelin, father and son, are a marvellous piece of representation, and so is the interior of the room where they are talking. That is a picture which will keep its interest for centuries. There was another picture by the same artist, entitled *Cast Shadows*, in which a very middle-class man, far from handsome, is expressing silent love and adoration for a very middle-class woman, far from pretty, and who does not seem encouraging. The representation of individuality was so powerful in that picture that it gave evidence of an extraordinary talent for portrait. M. Georges Claude has not the piquant originality of M. Friant, but he paints with quiet skill and a rare degree of good taste, as in the portrait of a young man with a short beard, in the costume of the sixteenth century, a picture that attains a perfection of its own kind more satisfactory than the restless and often reckless experiments of the new school.

PORTRAIT OF M. CÉSAR FRANCK. BY MLLE. RONGIER.

M. Weerts is a most skilful painter on a small scale, and his numerous portraits of gentlefolks show much keen observation of the upper classes in their ordinary aspects, with the kind of liveliness that they have in drawing-rooms, but nothing deeper.

The reader may be surprised that I have not yet spoken of portrait-painters so famous as Bonnat and Carolus Duran. One reason is that I mentioned both of them in THE PORTFOLIO for 1890 (page 249), not at length, but in a few words that did justice to their eminent position. Still, although nobody disputes their rank amongst contemporary painters, their work is less interesting for me just now than that of some less successful men, because

R

it does not indicate any new tendency in the French school. A portrait by Bonnat may be a marvellous representation of a man (that of Cardinal Lavigerie is really a masterpiece), but it opens no new path to art. The elements of that success, the strong representation of mature manhood with the dignity of high station, aided by the advantages of a stately costume, are all of them elements that may be found in the portraiture of the seventeenth century. Again, in many of Bonnat's portraits the background is meaningless—it is a space of shade to give relief to a light dress, and it is nothing more—but the meaningless background is neither novel nor desirable, except that it helps the painter to get rapidly through his work. Carolus Duran has reached that stage in the career of a successful portrait-painter when rapidity of performance is an object. We admire the facile skill, we know that only a most accomplished artist can ever attain it to that degree, and we acknowledge the almost magical power that gives substance and relief to a figure and its costume with a few decided strokes of the brush; but what is most striking in work of this character is personal and inimitable. The quieter merits of such a serious performance as the portrait of Gounod may be more profitable as an example to younger men. It is difficult, indeed, to attain any real novelty in an art that has been so much practised as portrait-painting. It so often carries us back to the past. One of the greatest successes of the year 1891 has been the profile portrait of the celebrated beauty, Madame Gautreau, unquestionably a fine work, but evidently inspired by the early Italians.

A French critic has said that it is not prudent to write about portraits for long together, as the subject easily becomes monotonous. I have selected as illustrations the portrait of César Franck by Mlle. Rongier and that of M. Crozier by Louis Galliac as examples of plain dealing with modern attitudes and costumes. The attitude of the musician is in my opinion remarkably fine, the other is at least easy and unaffected : both portraits are sound modern work. The costumes of children are often much easier to deal with than those of men. In the Salon of 1890 there was a *Portrait d'Enfant* by M. Mouchot which recalled the dignity and grace of Charles I., and in 1887 M. Lefebvre exhibited portraits of Mlle. Mary and Robert de G. which were beautifully composed and made a complete picture, the girl sitting on a garden-seat, the boy standing by her side.

PORTRAIT OF M. CROZIER.   BY L. GALLIAC.

The subject of landscape has not been entirely neglected in these papers, as I have already said something about it in connexion with Impressionism. The influence of the Impressionists has been very great, even outside of their own sect, and it may be fairly argued that their principle would be absolutely right in landscape-painting if it could be carried out successfully. It is in reality nothing more than effect-painting, which is the foundation of harmony in landscape and also the necessary condition of the expression of an artist's feeling. Accurate linear drawing of the forms of tangible objects, such as trees and rocks, excludes the expression of sentiment and is unfavourable to unity, whilst an effect almost ensures unity of itself, and excites an emotion in the artist which communicates itself to his work. We know that effect-painting is nothing new ; what is novel in the more recent French landscape-painters is their self-abandonment to the impression of the effect without stopping to consider whether they have knowledge enough to reproduce the entire scene. They refuse to eke out the scantiness of their knowledge by making use of materials got by careful object-drawing. Another characteristic of theirs is an extreme love for simplicity of subject. This is sometimes carried almost incredibly far, as when an artist gives you nothing but a broad expanse of pale sky reflected in calm water, with a line of misty distant shore between them. A more interesting but still very simple subject is this by M. Dainville, *On the Moorland*, where a clump of meagre trees has attracted him like an oasis in the desert. With all its simplicity it is not without some grace of composition. A very impressive picture by the same artist was *The Moor of San Marach*, exhibited in 1888, a dreary treeless expanse of moor rising to a stormy upland. These are very characteristic pictures, full of serious interest in a kind of nature that would discourage most landscape-painters by its dreariness. The French rivers have more charm, and they are heartily

ON THE MOORLAND. BY C. M. DAINVILLE.

appreciated by several artists of great merit. One of the best painters of river scenery is M. Nozal. His picture of *The Seine at St. Pierre, near Louviers, on an October Morning*, exhibited in the Salon of 1891, is a remarkably true and beautiful interpretation of a very difficult effect. The white moon is still visible in the grey sky and the mist is rising between us and a line of poplars and willows on the opposite shore, pale with distance, yet rich in autumnal colouring. The foreground was remarkable for the artist's success in the suggestion of early dew and even of gossamer, that cannot be painted. Another admirable work by the same artist was entitled *Storm-Clouds: the Pond of St. Quentin at Trappes, Seine et Oise*. As the title indicates, the principal subject of the picture is the sky, and it is a magnificent one, the clouds being in great masses of various greys, passing from dark to light and from cold to warmer colouring with a rare mastery of effect. There is strong light in the green land and the sandy shore and the rippling water. These pictures show quite as much knowledge of effect as those of the Impressionists, with more study of the materials of landscape. Other remarkable pictures are the strange and astonishing, yet, I believe, perfectly truthful representations of the coast of Provence by M. Olive. What seems to interest him most is the powerful contrast of colour in full sunshine between the deep blue waters and the arid rocks of desolate isle or shore—rocks that offer the most curious varieties of hue, from a warm white, glaring in the sunshine, to reds and browns that play together in reflections mingled with the deep azure water. Here is a painter who makes full use of the modern liberty to see the colouring of nature and to represent desolate scenery far from the experience of the Parisians. What outcries such landscape-painting would have excited in the middle of the present century! Now it hardly attracts the attention that it deserves. And whilst thinking of southern scenery I am reminded of the water-colours of Ruth Mercier, which show a remarkable knowledge of colour and tone in combination with an uncommonly summary execution and a manual power of the kind best suited for water-colour. Oil painting does not seem to display her talent equally well, because much of the charm of her work consists in the sure skill displayed in the broad washes. It is a most intelligent kind of performance, without any useless labour, yet expressive of all that is characteristic in the beautiful southern landscape amongst which the artist lives and works. Ruth Mercier does not always seek to express the desolation of the south ; she can treat a distant town with as much interest as if she were, like Turner, essentially a painter of distant cities : yet perfectly wild nature interests her also, as when she sits down to make a masterly study of the ghastly rocks on the Ile Sainte Marguerite, with nothing but the dark blue water beyond them and the flying clouds above. The artist is also great in flower-painting, and it is possible that constant practice from flowers may have developed her naturally good perception of colour whilst giving facility of hand.

I hope it is permissible to admire the most opposite qualities in art ; if it is not per-missible, few critics expose themselves to the charge of inconsistency more frequently than I. There is nothing in common between the work of Ruth Mercier and that of M. Binet, except that both are perfectly sincere. The most striking characteristics of the first are comprehensiveness of conception and breadth of execution ; the distinguishing talent of the second is observation. M. Binet paints exactly like a clever and observant Englishman. He is not at all an Impressionist—far from it ; and I fear that the absence of poetic charm and glamour will prevent him from attaining any great celebrity ; but few living painters approach him in the honest representation of nature, with equal attention to form and colour. There is never any daubing in Binet's work, as there is in so much French landscape—never any attempt to substitute mere paint for the complex and intricate truth of nature. His interest in what he sees is too equal for any striking special characteristic ; but I should say that while in his nearer and more confined scenery he may be compared with other careful draughtsmen, he is more alone in his capacity for painting extensive views. An example of this faculty is a recent picture of *The Great Pond at St. Aubin, near Quilleboeuf*, which is not only full of careful study, but lays before us an extensive tract of country. Another very thorough student of nature is M. Isenbart, of Besançon, whom I have mentioned in a former chapter. His two contributions to the Salon of 1891 were hung in a place of honour, in the principal room of the exhibition. They were illustrations of the delightful scenery amongst which he has passed his life. No river in France is more pictorial than the Doubs that winds around the fortress - city of Besançon, like the Tagus about Toledo, and the Doubs never had a more faithful or more capable student than M. Isenbart. Here again, however, as in the case of M. Binet, there is too much of nature in the work for a predominant artistic reputation. In the pictures of the great celebrities—Claude, Turner, Corot—there is much more than nature. The healthy brightness of M. Isenbart's work is also rather against him so far as great reputation is concerned, because he never seems solemn or profound. No one has painted the autumnal colour of eastern France more faithfully than he.

M. Lepère is an artist of great versatility and originality. He is at the same time a painter, a clever original etcher, and what is still rarer, an original wood-engraver of un-

Storm Clouds.

common talent and skill. As a landscape-painter he varies almost as much as the moods of Nature herself. His colour is sometimes glaring (as in *L'Oise près de Vauréal, le Lavoir*), and sometimes extremely sober, according to the effect in nature. Some of his pictures must seem outrageous to those who have fixed ideas about nature and art, and who find in the monotony of Corot or Claude a sufficient translation of the external world. I know that M. Lepère's work is sometimes rough and crude, but he sees relations of colour in nature— such as the play of blues, greens, and purples in the light and shadows on a river—which the masters of what is considered correct landscape never had the courage to attempt at all ; whilst instead of giving himself up exclusively to the brighter colouring of nature, he takes just as much

THE SOURCE OF THE OISELLE. BY TANCRÈDE ABRAHAM.

interest in the gold and brown of late evening or in the greys of a colder twilight and the russets of the earth—as in *The Valley of the Oise at Jouy-le-Moutier*. M. Lepère is a member of the National Society of Fine Arts ; a few years ago colouring as frank as his would have ensured rejection from any French exhibition. Another landscape-painter whose name, Lepine, is similar enough to create a possible confusion, keeps much more within a certain habitual range, both of colour and execution. His skies are usually luminous with light blues and greys, and the greens of his foliage and herbage are pleasantly broken. His execution appears to be a tradition from Constable, and his choice of subjects is amongst quiet lowland river and canal scenery, except when he takes us to such a moderate elevation as the Parisian hill of Montmartre. His pictures are harmonious in themselves and when seen together, but are not likely to excite either passionate enthusiasm or any loud antagonism. They are true in effect, though without accuracy of form. An equally quiet colourist, more studious of form, is M. Tancrède Abraham. Both these artists have certainly that poetical element which is so valuable to the landscape-painter. A practical advantage of quiet colouring, like that of M. Abraham, is that it can be hung safely in almost any room, whereas violent colour, though equally true to nature, asserts itself too much for pleasant permanent companionship. The more famous French landscape-painter, Harpignies, is also a very quiet colourist with a poetic senti-ment. His two subjects of *Dawn* and *Sunset*, in the Salon of 1891, would have afforded a good pretext for splendour ; but he restrained himself with the utmost discretion, preferring tender grey-

s

greens with a distance of purple or rose.   Both works were perfectly harmonious in themselves, but the work was arrested at a point previous to what in England would be called 'finish.'

One of the very few landscape-painters quite of the modern school, whose work combines truth of colour with a sense of elegance in drawing, is M. Louis Le Camus.   All his pictures from the South of France seem to me delightful.   One of the best (Champ-de-Mars, 1891) is entitled *The Sea-shore at Cape Martin*.   The sea is intensely purple, and there is a very fine and truthful study of reddish mountain.   As a colourist, M. Le Camus has the rare merit of being sober or brilliant when necessary, without attaching himself systematically either to dulness of hue, like the old French landscape-painters, or to glare, like some modern Impressionists—such, for example, as Montenard, whose constant efforts towards truth in glaring southern sunshine I would not, however, undervalue.   Whilst few modern pictures are so powerful as *The Sea-shore at Cape Martin*, few are so delicate as that by the same artist entitled *Under the Olive Woods at the Close of Day*, and *Evening amongst the Lemon-trees*.   I have said that M. Le Camus painted a mountainous coast well.   Very few Frenchmen have attacked mountainous scenery with success.   Although within France itself there are extensive ranges of the finest mountainous scenery in Europe, equal to the best

EVENING AT DRUILLAT.   BY A. RAPIN.

in Switzerland or in Spain, landscape-painters have hitherto almost exclusively confined themselves to the lowlands.   One exception is M. Balouzet, of Lyons, who paints the most desolate Alpine scenery with great truth—as, for example, in his picture of *The Riffel Lake, near Zermatt*, in the Salon of 1891.   This does not prevent M. Balouzet from doing justice to the quiet motives of lowland scenery, as in his *October Evening at Poncins on the Loire*, in the same exhibition — a picture with great breadth of rather sombre and melancholy effect, recalling rather the best French landscape-painting of thirty years ago than the present energetic school.

How quickly the new passes into the old !   In a few years the glare of French Impressionism will be as much a thing of the past as that of English Pre-Raphaelitism is to-day.   The leaders of the French landscape of ten years ago are now either dead or *démodés*.   Two eminent Frenchmen died quite recently who but yesterday were leading men in the school.   Rapin, notwithstanding his unlucky name, was an artist of great breadth of conception, able to carry out a transient effect over a large canvas, but not always selecting those effects in nature which are best adapted to the purposes of art.   Pelouse, by his powerful execution in the representation of near scenery and his knowledge of effect in, the more extensive landscapes that he painted occasionally, won for himself a strong and latterly, unassailable position in the school.   His career was crowned by the magnificent display of his works in the Universal Exhibition of 1889.   I have not space to expatiate on those works in detail, and, indeed, feel strongly the uselessness of disquisitions on pictures that the reader may not have seen, or may fail to remember.

I had intended, in the present chapter, to say something about marine-painting in France, but for want of space must restrict myself to a single observation. The most modern

EMBARKATION OF M. CARNOT ON THE 'FORMIDABLE.' BY A. BRUN.

painters do not at all shrink from the unpicturesque ironclad or the passenger steamer, or the too neat and pretty yachts and little boats. As an example of skill in dealing with a very difficult subject I give a sketch from M. Brun's picture of the *Embarkation of M. Carnot on the 'Formidable'* when he went to Corsica. It seems to me that M. Brun has entirely overcome the difficulty, and that the picture (exhibited in the Salon of 1891) is so composed as to impress us with the majesty of a war-ship that deserves its terrible name.

X

Sculpture

A WELL-KNOWN French critic said that if he followed his own impulses he would give himself as much space for sculpture as for painting in his reviews of the annual exhibitions, but the greater public interest in pictures made such a distribution of space impossible. The French critic's wish for room to speak of sculpture would hardly occur to an Englishman in England, because there the art of painting is predominant as much in merit and in vitality as it is in popularity. In France, notwithstanding the evident skill and power of the painters, it might be argued that the sculptors are, at least, their equals, and that the school of modern sculpture is as much alive as the school of painting, and as full of promise for the future. And, although undoubtedly the majority of French people care more for pictures than they do for statues, still there is a minority that takes an equal interest in sculpture, and I myself have known French people who had a special and peculiar interest in plastic art, of a kind that is excessively rare in England. There is, indeed, something in plastic art that answers to the genius of the French mind. Architecture is a living art in France, and when architecture lives sculpture of some kind is always sure to live with it. The modern architectural taste of the French mind is essentially classical; it has revived Gothic as an archaeological and ecclesiastical study, but when left to itself its expression is sure to be classical. The French would never think of building Gothic Houses of Parliament: the idea would never occur to them. Now, a classical taste in architecture is always accompanied by the desire for perfection in sculpture; it is accompanied by an ambition that looks beyond mere decorative carving, beyond the carving of rude and picturesque ornament which was sufficiently accomplished to satisfy Gothic architects, but is not learned enough for the successors of the Greeks. Besides this, any one who knows the French well must be aware that in all matters of culture they are very willing to submit to discipline, and that they take the fine arts very seriously—that their painting, at least of the human figure, is founded upon the hard and patient study of form. With these qualities they are likely enough to produce good sculptors, and they have naturally the plastic instinct, without which the best of training is but a waste of time.

The instinct must indeed be irresistible when it leads so many young men to enter a profession in which there are hardly any clients except a few public bodies and the State. Here and there a Duke of Aumale, or a Duke of Luynes, buys statues, and smaller folks may commission a bust or a medallion, but there is no purchasing public in France, and the sculptor looks to the foreign magnate or the American millionaire. The life of a sculptor is hard and anxious. I remember Gautherin before he rose to fame—what a terrible life he led, toiling beyond his strength, living like an anchorite, fighting the hard battle that led to a few short years of celebrity and a premature grave. And the unsuccessful men, clever enough to exhibit in the Salon but doing no business, the wonder is that they go on from year to year. I went to see one of them last winter, and found him in a poor workshop in an obscure street, carving by the light of one dim lamp and earning his bread by un-

The Sleep of the Child Jesus, from the Sculpture by Antoine Garlet.

interesting task-work. Many of them carve ornaments for tombstones, or climb scaffoldings to chisel brackets under balconies.

Amidst these numerous failures it is pleasant to come upon a deserved success. The group by Antoine Joseph Gardet, *The Sleep of the Child Jesus*, was one of the great successes in the Salon of 1891. The technical skill and knowledge displayed in the work made it satisfactory to artists, the religious public were pleased and touched by the chastity and serenity of the conception, whilst the popular taste was gratified by the delightful way in which the artist had both realised and idealised the charm of infancy in its two states of watchful wakefulness and unconscious rest. The mother, too, commanded respect by her dignity and grace, accompanied by that gravity, verging upon sadness, which belongs properly to one called to a painful and exceptional maternity. However frivolous and corrupt our age may be, the most serious art is still the surest of success. Perhaps in this instance the seriousness of the artist's temper may have been enhanced by his own presentiment that this would be his 'last word' in art. The group appeared in the Salon with the piece of crape by which the critic knows that his praise is useless. Few artists have ended a brief career more happily, or left a fairer monument.

Antoine Gardet was a pupil of Aimé Millet and Cavelier. There is another Gardet, Georges, a pupil of Millet and Frémiet, who has a sound knowledge of animals, and much sympathy with them. The range of his interest in animals extends from the tragedy of the great carnivora to the tender innocence of the inexperienced little chick or duckling. In the Universal Exhibition of 1889 he exhibited a bear in marble and a group of wild animals in bronze; in the

DANISH DOG. BY G. GARDET.

Salon of the same year he had a *Danish Dog* in marble, and in 1891 his whole 'exposition' consisted of a tiny chick and a duckling in marble, both of them full of the closest observation. This may not be very high art, perhaps—and, indeed, it belongs partly to natural history—but the greatest French sculptors do not disdain the study of animals when they have an affection for them. M. Frémiet is unquestionably one of the greatest sculptors now living in Europe, and there is nothing that he enjoys more than the contrast between human and animal form. In 1885 he exhibited a group entitled *Bear and Man in the Stone Age*. The man has killed a cub and wounded the mother, who, standing on her hind-legs, is wrestling with him, and has got him in her fatal grip. He is strong, yet powerless against the superior strength of the beast, and his wit avails him nothing. The same idea of human powerlessness before superior animal force was expressed in another and still more tragical group, exhibited in 1887, and entitled simply *Gorilla*. The terrible beast has carried off a woman that he holds easily with one long hairy arm, whilst she struggles and pushes vainly. With the other arm he has picked up a large stone that he is ready to throw with his superhuman strength, as he gazes steadfastly at his enemies. The subject is horrible, but the strength of invention, both in general conception and in fearfully significant detail, was beyond dispute, and no one was surprised when the jury awarded M. Frémiet the medal of honour. What a strange power this faculty of artistic invention is! No living sculptor has it in greater strength than M. Frémiet. In the Salon of 1891 there was a bronze statuette by him of an old subject, *St. George slaying the Dragon*. The group was full of vital invention from beginning to end, even to the bending back of the lance as the horse had carried the rider a little beyond his mark. I was admiring the consistent invention of the Dragon, in company with one of the most distinguished members of the jury who knew Frémiet well, and he told me that the grisly beast had been suggested to the sculptor by the back of a skinned rabbit. Here is the difference between imaginative power and the lack of it. To a housekeeper a skinned rabbit suggests nothing but a mediocre dish; to the great sculptor it suggests the legendary enemy of St. George! It is curious how the different studies of an artist sometimes tend to combine themselves in a single work. M. Frémiet has executed several equestrian statues in armour, as, for example, his *Grand Condé* (1881) and his *Jeanne d'Arc*. We have seen that he has also studied fierce animals. The two are combined in the St. George.

Another great inventive sculptor is M. Rodin, also unquestionably a man of genius, not so sober or so severely cultured as M. Frémiet, but still more imaginative, one of the

ALSATIA AND LORRAINE. BY M. BARTHOLDI.

very few artists of the present day who may, without presumption, undertake the illustration of Dante. His great Dante door, as yet unfinished, is wonderful for exuberance of imagination. In everything that M. Rodin does there is an intensity of perception, a grasp of the subject, that put his sign-manual on every bone and muscle. I saw in a friend's house a bronze fragment of a man's trunk and knew it at once to be by Rodin. 'Yes,' said the owner, 'it was a bit of work in clay begun and thrown aside, so I got leave to have it cast in bronze.' His portraits are not flattering, but they are full of character and prove his interest in the life-history of a man. No artist marks more observedly the effects of years, of thought, labour, anxiety. His finest busts are those of elderly men who have gone through much hard intellectual work. One of the best is the recent one of Puvis de Chavannes; the statue of Victor Hugo in the monument for the Pantheon (as yet only a sketch) is at the same time a likeness and a peculiar kind of idealisation quite different from classical embellishments of form. M. Rodin even takes a curious interest in the hideous. He showed me a terrible statuette, in bronze, too dreadful for exhibition, which was simply an attempt to express the hideousness of old age. He had got some wretched old woman to pose for him, and the result, with his own powerful accentuation, was a fearful perfection of ugliness, fascinating in its own way, for I found it hardly possible to turn away from it.

AGRIPPA D'AUBIGNÉ WHEN A BOY.
BY RAMBAUD.

I only know M. Bartholdi's *Liberty lighting the World* by the reduced copy erected at Paris. It is majestic even in the reduction, but every statue is conceived for its own intended scale, and we can hardly judge of the enormous when reduced to the simply colossal. The Eiffel Tower, reduced to the height of a church steeple, would not be the Eiffel Tower. I prefer, therefore, to estimate M. Bartholdi by what I have seen in its full dimensions; for example, the marble group of *Alsatia and Lorraine taking Refuge at the Altar of 'la Patrie,'* intended for Gambetta's monument at Ville d'Avray. If the whole monument may be judged from this part of it, our only regret must be that it was not erected in place of the foolish composition that occupies the finest site in Paris, between the Louvre and the Place du Carrousel. The figures in M. Bartholdi's group are well composed, with sufficient variety to exclude an excessive formality, and they are really living, both in attitude and expression. The allegory is good enough for a sculptor's use, though the refuge offered by the French 'Patrie' to the lost provinces is one of which they are not at liberty to avail themselves, so that their satisfaction is purely ideal. Monumental sculpture has made several very important contributions to the Salons of recent years. In 1888 M. Bartholdi exhibited his monument to Paul Bert, which was original enough in the heavy architectural forms that sustained the

recumbent figure, the head falling back in death, whilst the left hand grasped the tricolour and the right hung down by the side of the marble couch. The drapery resembled that of an ancient Roman, the legs and feet bare and also the left arm. The makers of ecclesiastical monuments are more fortunate in the matter of draperies when they have to immortalise a prelate, and the poor *curé* seldom gets immortalised in marble.

An arrangement usually adopted for great Church dignitaries is to make them kneel in full canonicals, with a train behind them and a mitre and crozier on the ground, as in M. Vasselot's Bishop Lamazou (1888) and the portrait of Archbishop Landriot by M. Thomas (1880). Exactly the same arrangement was adopted ten years later by M. Delaplanche for the monument to Bishop Donnet. It is too convenient to go out of fashion, as it combines piety with magnificence and the insignia of rank. It also affords to the sculptor an opportunity for the display of his skill in such

MONUMENT TO DANTON. BY PARIS.

things as draperies and lace. So in the monument to the Count de Chambord by M. Caravannier, exhibited in 1888: the heir of the Bourbons was represented in his royal mantle, sprinkled with *fleurs-de-lis*, as he knelt on one knee with the crown of France on a cushion close to his foot. For my part I look back rather regretfully to these splendours and dignities of a time now fading rapidly into the past. The royalty of Henri V. was so shadowy that it is hardly remembered, and even his best adherents do not visit his grave. How vain the

THE SEWER-MAN.
BY M. MATHIEU-MEUSNIER.

marble crown and mantle, imitating the gold and velvet that he never wore! In the touching group of Louis Philippe and Queen Amélie, by Mercié, exhibited in 1866, and now in the chapel at Dreux, the Queen is kneeling, whilst the King stands erect in the royal mantle, his left hand placed affectionately on her shoulder: they two belong to 'ancient history,' as the French say, and the pair have a melancholy expression on their faces, as if they were thinking that their royalty had been ephemeral and a failure. The Orleans family have a taste for good monumental sculpture, and are willing to pay for the finest work of this kind that can be produced. Their chapel at Dreux has the double interest of a curious historical memorial and a collection of admirable monumental art. The most splendid of royal monuments do not remain in the memory so well as something that touches us. M. Mercié exhibited in 1885 a marble, entitled *Souvenir*, a statue of regretful Recollection seated against a tomb—certainly one of the most pathetic works in modern art, enough to awaken in each of us the memories that are associated with our dead. Some years ago M. de Saint Marceau had a brilliant success with his *Genius guarding the Secret of the Tomb*, that secret which is so well guarded.

French sculptors are now more than ever employed on statues of famous men, of course with the ever-recurring difficulty of modern costume, which they either avoid ingeniously or grapple with audaciously. M. Thiers is a very

PORTRAIT OF M. SOISSON. BY RINGEL D'ILLZACH.

difficult subject for a statue, partly on account of his physical insignificance, but mainly because he never wore a costume that was good for anything in sculpture. The most typical instance of modern costume in French sculpture is the statue of M. Aristide Boucicaut, the great shop-keeper, by M. Leroux. M. Boucicaut, of course, dressed in the usual frock-coat, waistcoat, and trousers; but as the sculptor wished to avoid the prim neatness of a fashion card he made the clothes fit badly, so that M. Boucicaut seemed to have got into a coat too big for him. The attitude, with one hand in his pocket and the other on his cane, seemed to call for the completion of a hat, but this the sculptor did not venture upon. The statue was, I believe, a good likeness. To us it is interesting chiefly as an attempt to deal with the most unrewarding of all possible costumes. It is useless to struggle against the fatal difficulty of dress. One of the most justly famous statues of modern times is the *Florentine Singer of the Fifteenth Century*, by Dubois, at present in the Luxembourg. The costume is extremely simple—tight hose, a shirt with narrow sleeves, a sort of waistcoat, and a belt. This comes next to the nude as permitting the study of form. The robes of a prelate or sovereign may hide the form, but they substitute a wealth of drapery In the *bourgeois* dress of M. Boucicaut there is neither form nor drapery.

The costume of the sixteenth century combines form with an element of the picturesque. We have it in Rambaud's statue of *Agrippa d'Aubigné when a Boy*. From the outstretched hand it may be supposed that he is taking the oath his father required of him in presence of the gibbeted Protestants at Amboise. His boyhood deserved a statue, being at the same time most accomplished and most brave. M. Rambaud's work was worthy of so noble a subject, being both graceful and serious. We know by the works of Meissonier that the costume of the eighteenth century is well adapted to painting—as well, indeed, as any costume can be. Many contemporary sculptors go back to it with equal satisfaction. The most important of all recent efforts in this direction was the large panel in high relief by Dalou, illustrating the famous reply of Mirabeau to the Marquis de Dreux-Brézé, 'Go and tell your master that we are here by the will of the people, and that we will leave only if turned out with bayonets.' This great work has been placed in the Chamber of Deputies, where it may be present in scenes equally stormy if not quite so important in the history of France. A quieter work by the same artist, also with the costume

ARLEQUINE. BY FOSSÉ.

of the eighteenth century, is the thoughtful figure of Lavoisier, with legs crossed, the elbow resting on the knee, the chin on the hand, now on the Boulevard St. Germain. The face of this statue might be taken as a typical illustration of abstract thinking.

THE CAT OF THE REGIMENT. BY MADAME TOUZIN.

The *Danton*, by M. Paris, is an equally fine example of inspiration to action. The democratic leader looks vulgar but determined, and the bronze itself seems to bawl even as he probably bawled. It is a trick of sculptors in compositions of this kind to put figures crouching on each side of the principal one. Few groups of the kind have been more animated than this of *Danton*. That was democratic art on its heroic side; but the same democratic or plebeian spirit that I have already noticed in much modern French painting is visible in sculpture also. The ideal of form is often abandoned as the artist's aim in favour of human interest, as for example in the *Sewerman* by M. Mathieu-Meusnier, whose enormous boots conceal form effectually, and the real interest of the statue is in the quiet courage of the face and attitude. This idea of celebrating and admiring those who do the world's most disagreeable work is essentially a democratic idea. There was a group by M. Theunissen in the Salon of 1891, entitled *During the Strike*, and representing a poor family depressed by hunger and saddened by the wretched look-out before them. Beauty, of course, and any notion of idealisation, were quite outside of the artist's

aim, which was purely to excite sympathy with the working class, and in this he succeeded. Still, it seems to me that when pathetic interest is entirely severed from beauty it belongs rather to the province of painting, which has compensations in colour and light-and-shade.

When a sculptor likes character more than anything, the most various motives may set him to work. I have not yet seen the statue of Queen Mary Stuart by M. Ringel d'Illzach, but hope he has done justice to her beauty. I cannot admire *La Parisienne*, by the same sculptor, except for its observation. It was marvellously vulgar. A woman in evening dress was seated with one arm on the back of her chair, and her legs crossed, the foot on the ground being turned so that she rested on the side of it, with the inevitable ugly bend in the ankle. The head, craning forward, had an unpleasantly impudent expression. But what vitality! The woman was so much alive that we wanted her to hold herself better. The same remarkable vitality and individuality of character are visible in all M. Ringel's medallion portraits, by this time very numerous. Speaking of modern subjects in sculpture, I notice that the bicyclists have found their artist in M. H. Dubois, who celebrates their prowess on medallions, showing how well adapted their costume is to artistic treatment of rather a severe kind. Its extreme neatness and conformity to the human shape make it seem classical when treated in a classical spirit. This is a curious instance of the rapidity with which the fine arts adopt things of recent introduction. Even the machines did well in the medallions.

The contrast between the classical and the popular ways of treating similar subjects has rarely been better marked than between the severe and graceful beauty of the finely draped *Danseuse*, by Chapu, in the Salon of 1890, and the *Arlequine* of M. Fossé in that of 1891. The first was highly idealised, and so carefully wrought out in every curve of flesh and drapery as to have acquired the interest of inexhaustible beauty. The second is extremely true, lively, and French—pretty, too, in its own way, but, of course, considerably below the region of the ideal. If this subject seems rather frivolous we are not to conclude that the artist is incapable of deep and even tragic sympathies. He exhibited in 1866 a group representing a mother, a plain woman of the people, holding the naked body of a boy, her son, across her knees, killed by two bullets in the massacre of the Second of December. The stern, deep misery of the mother was expressed with imposing truth and power. The army has become much more popular since it has been national, and is now a frequent subject for friendly treatment by sculptors, as in the vigorous group of fighting recruits by M. Croisy (1885), entitled *The Army of the Loire*, and in many affectionately trivial illustrations of military life in its details, such, for example, as Madame Touzin's *Cat of the Regiment*, where a cat perches behind a Zouave's neck whilst he gravely marches on.

JUPILLE, THE SHEPHERD, AND THE MAD DOG. BY TRUFFOT.

The realism which has invaded modern French sculpture is an advantage in the treatment of children and animals, as they rarely have any severe dignity, yet are full of delightful interest in a thousand trivial motions that seem beneath the attention of high art. I was delighted with the lively happiness of three children in a bronze group by M. Louis Martin (1891), entitled *After School*. They are running and skipping, hand in hand, in the most exuberant glee. An opportunity for seizing upon the tragic side of boyish and animal life was afforded by the incident of the shepherd-boy Jupille, who battled very courageously with a mad dog, muzzling him with his whip. The boy was bitten, and afterwards successfully treated by M. Pasteur, the first trial of his method on a human subject, an experiment that caused the *savant* the most intense anxiety. Two sculptors tried the subject at the same time. Of the two, M. Truffot showed the stronger sense of the situation. His group was exhibited in 1887.

The greatest of all living sculptors of animals is unquestionably M. Cain. Whilst most others are men of more or less talent, Cain is a man of genius. His groups are not merely illustrations of natural history, but works of consummate art. In the Salon of 1891 there was a magnificent bronze by him representing *Eagles and Vultures quarrelling over a dead Bear*. The expression of life and conflict in the birds — the eagle majestic, the vulture envious and hostile, and also the deathful hanging and drooping of the bear — were as good as anything in the finest works of Barye, whilst the sense of composition displayed in the whole group lifted it far above the range of simple realism. A less important work by the same artist, *Dogs Tied Up* (1887), showed intimate knowledge of more familiar animals.

DOGS TIED UP. BY CAIN.

There are many inevitable omissions in this chapter. A medium between modern democratic art which celebrates labourers in their ordinary dress, and the serene art of classic times that glorifies dignity and repose, may be found in the fine colossal nude figure, in marble, which M. Alfred Boucher has entitled *La Terre*. It is a man of gigantic strength, toiling with a spade, and with sufficient effort to display all his muscular development. There is a tendency in modern sculpture to occupy itself with other materials than the usual marble and bronze. The recumbent figure of a martyr carved in wood by M. Bloch was absolutely first-rate work, and amongst the *objets d'art* exhibited in the Champ-de-Mars were some pieces of furniture by M. Carabin with very little ornament in metal and wood, but that of rare excellence, including well-carved figures. But of all recent technical experiments I know of none so interesting as the works in coloured glass by M. Henry Cros. They are coloured, opaque, and perfectly dead in surface though vitrified, having a peculiar and exquisite quality. The discovery of the process, which I am unable to explain in detail, has cost the author the most prolonged and pertinacious labour. He employs it for works in low or high relief, such as medallions and plaques, of which he exhibited a remarkable collection in 1889. M. Cros is himself a delicate colourist with a scrupulously refined taste, and in hands as capable as his I have no doubt that the new art might be introduced with excellent effect in modern architectural decoration.

Architecture

THE interest of France as a country for the study of architecture is that the art is alive there and national, not seeking its models in any foreign contemporary school, and treating those of the past with the freedom that belongs to complete independence. This could not, I believe, be said with equal truth of any other country. There is not in Europe, and there is still less in America, any country whose architecture borrows so little from abroad, or adapts itself with so much freedom and elegance to the varying necessities of the present. In saying this, I am not unmindful of the good and original work produced by several English architects of the present day. There is, no doubt, a great variety and vitality of conception in contemporary English work, and the general artistic advancement in England is probably leading to a great architectural future; but taking the two countries just as they are at the present moment, and not looking too far ahead, I think it is indisputable that France produces architecture more easily and naturally, as well as in greater abundance. For example, a block of buildings like Queen Anne's Mansions would not have been erected in Paris. The pervading architectural sense of the place would have urged the builders to attempt something more than a

HOUSE IN THE RUE DU LUXEMBOURG, PARIS.
M. Cahn Bousson, Architect.

lofty brick box, with oblong holes in it for windows. The problem of the big house to be let in flats is one that has engaged the attention of French architects for many years, and it is important enough in a modern capital to deserve all the care and intelligence that can be brought to bear upon it.

The reader is perhaps familiar with the common criticisms on the Rue de Rivoli, especially on that part of it which extends from the Ministère de la Marine to the Rue du Louvre. Had it not been for the variety given to one side of the street by the Louvre and Tuileries, the monotony of it would have been as bad as the monotony of Harley Street, though the masonry is more costly and better finished. The mechanical repetition of the same arch, balcony, and windows, in an apparently infinite perspective, can have no better effect than that so easily attained by putting two looking-glasses on opposite walls of a room. It is multiplication, and no more. There is no reason for stopping anywhere to see any particular arch or any window when those before us are precisely exact copies of those we have left behind. Not that the builders of the Rue de Rivoli are to be condemned as if they had invented repetition. We had it already in Greek architecture, and in Gothic, but with this difference, that the old architects always knew where to stop. No Greek would have made an apparently unending array of columns, no Gothic builder would have made a cathedral a mile long. And the modern French themselves have, architecturally, now left the Rue de Rivoli far behind them. It is now a long time since that street was built. It was finished in 1855, and in the thirty-six years that have elapsed since then all the fine arts have gained greatly in variety and interest. The fault least readily forgiven in the present day is dulness, and it is not easy to prevent a lofty tenement house from being dull. The mere height of it is in itself a great difficulty, especially as the division into floors leaves no liberty for a corresponding height of windows. When such a problem is dealt with inartistically the result is Queen Anne's Mansions.

A good example of the Parisian solution of the same problem is a house in the Rue du Luxembourg by M. Cahn Bousson. To prevent emptiness and sameness in the great expanse of height, it is divided into distinct parts. The ground floor and first story are taken together with alternate courses of stones rusticated and all joints deeply incised. This part of the structure ends with a heavy stone balcony with a balustrade supported by four deep and massive carved consoles. Above this the masonry is plain and smooth, and the balconies of the third and fourth floors have light iron railings. The cornice, instead of being quite at the top of the building, as in Italian architecture, is ingeniously brought down

CONSOLES AND BALCONY ON THE FOURTH STORY.
M. Cahn Bousson, Architect.

almost to two-sevenths of the total height,* by having a story between it and the beginning of the roof, whilst a story is gained in the roof itself by the slight inclination of the lower rafters.† By this device the house proper is made to finish apparently at the cornice, where the balcony has a stone balustrade, and all above is but a light, plain superstructure. In some of the most recent Parisian houses this superstructure is made of distinctly different materials, so as to seem rather a thing erected upon the house than a part of the house itself. It is hardly necessary to observe that the variety in the balconies (in the present instance very ingenious) is intended to be of use in the division of the mass. Of late years a kind of light oriel window has been frequently introduced in Parisian houses. It includes two or three stories, and is supported by consoles, or by a stone cul-de-lampe, which affords a good opportunity for sculpture. The framework of the window may be of oak or iron, and the glass is usually in small panes, leaded. The effect from the street is picturesque, as these

---

* This is not apparent on the perspective view, but it is obvious on the elevation.
† Fifteen degrees from the vertical. In Mansard roofs (so called from the French architect who invented them) there are two sets of rafters, A B and B C, instead of one set, A C, as in the older system of roofing.

projecting windows break the monotony of the front. The gain to the interior is very great. In the small Parisian rooms a few square feet make the difference between confinement and a sense of space. The idea is borrowed from the projecting lattices of Arab architecture, cleverly adapted to that of modern Paris, and it may safely be predicted that projecting windows will be more employed in the future and with a richer variety of design. The desire for more interesting or (as a French artist would call it) more amusing architecture is seen not only in the present extensive employment of coloured or tinted glass in small panes, or moulded with facets like jewels, but also in the now frequent insertion of coloured slabs of pottery, which give opportunities for an endless variety of decoration and are not affected by smoke, of which there is more in Paris than there used to be. Ceramic decoration associates itself very easily and naturally with the new iron architecture (of which

VILLA, BOULEVARD DE BOULOGNE, SEINE.
M. Lucien Magne, Architect.

I shall have more to say presently), and it is often used for villas and other private houses that aim rather at being pretty and interesting than imposing.

Before passing to these, I wish the reader to take note that although there are many very accomplished architects in Paris and in other French cities, who never turn out work that is not, at least, designed with some intelligence and care, France also abounds in a class of builders who are simply masons without artistic culture of any kind, yet whose work bears some superficial resemblance to that of architects and may cast discredit on French culture, though in reality

French culture has nothing whatever to do with it. Their work is not exactly that of the London jerry-builder — it is more substantial and may be durable enough ; the misfortune about it is that so much fairly good handicraft should not have been employed in the realisation of an acceptable design. Some of the chapters of this volume were written in a Parisian street where building was going forward on the opposite side. The workmanship was excellent, the art deplorable, and the more to be lamented that any competent architect might have corrected it in a few minutes. On making inquiry I discovered that the houses were built by a master-mason as an investment, he being his own architect. I was told that he had become wealthy, and built many large houses for himself. In the provinces there is a dread of employing competent architects on account of their supposed costliness, and this perhaps may be a reason why some architects of great merit have applied their minds to the conciliation of art with economy. M. Bocage has successfully attempted this in five different and independent houses, perfectly architectural, with quite sufficient ornament, yet costing only 1120*l.* each, everything included. Notwithstanding the higher rate of wages in Paris, I doubt whether houses of that quality could be built for so little in any French country town. I have been rather surprised by the costliness of building in the provinces, where 3000*l.* or 4000*l.* is a common outlay for a house of no great pretensions. A good example of a cheap, yet artistic and picturesque villa, is one by M. Lucien Magne on the Boulevard de Boulogne. In this case the chief economies are in the extreme simplicity of the masonry and in the absence of carving, either in stone or wood, whilst the picturesque elements are in the treatment of the openings and porches, in the use of visible carpentry, and in the judicious employment of ceramic decoration. There is often much fanciful irregularity in these villas. I remember one, at Passy, by M. Lheureux, where the architect's purpose was to make the most of an irregular corner of ground, to amuse and interest the eye as much as possible at a small expense. He seems to have taken a hint from the round towers of some old castle, but he adapted his idea entirely to modern requirements, one great semicircular projection being, in fact, a sort of conservatory, whilst a small round tower or turret is useful mainly as giving an apex to the composition. I never saw a happier example of the invented picturesque. M. Lheureux made use of everything—outside stairs, railings in unexpected places, massive shade given by verandah under the conservatory, an intricacy of thin linear detail in ironwork; but very little decoration, except two or three pieces of sculpture (some carving about a window or a fountain, or the capital of a column), and a course of coloured *faïences* under the roof of the round turret and that of an ivied building to the left of it.

Considering that Gothic architecture is essentially a French style, and that the French once excelled in it, and have studied it profoundly in the present century, it may seem strange that it has never been adopted for large tenement houses, and very rarely for public buildings other than ecclesiastical. The French usually prefer Gothic for churches after making various experiments in other styles, of which the Madeleine is the best-known example. It is not so much the architects who insist on Gothic churches as the clergy and laity. There are, however, good reasons for believing

CHURCH AT SOUVERAIN-MOULIN.
M. E. Duthoit, Architect.

that this preference is a mistake, except where money is abundant. For village churches nothing is practically so good as the French Romanesque—what is called in French *le Roman.* It is substantial, durable, and moderate in cost, whilst its homely, snug, and unpretending character makes it admirably adapted for use in villages. It is, however, exactly this unpretending character that the ambitious *curé* dislikes. He wants especially a tall church with a steeple, and neglects the beautiful and harmonious models of romanesque architecture that abound in old villages for the cheap Gothic of the contemporary architect. Sometimes, when the architect is skilful, he may solve the difficult problem of making Gothic acceptable and cheap at the same time. This seems to have been accomplished by M. Duthoit (a disciple of Viollet-le-Duc) in a little village church at Souverain-Moulin, which is remarkably complete, betrays no sign of parsimony, is by no means uninteresting or vacant in design, and yet only cost, including furniture, the almost incredibly small sum of 3000*l*. The church is of brick, with stone facings and ornaments, and there is even a little sculpture in conspicuous positions.

A good romanesque church has been built lately at Châteauroux (Indre) by M. A. Dauvergne. The only objection I feel inclined to make to it, and to others of the same type, is that romanesque architecture, when treated in this sense, tends to lose something of that sturdy strength which properly belongs to it, and to borrow something of the elegance of Gothic. For example, in the construction of towers and spires, the prevalent spirit of early French romanesque architecture is not to seek a great elevation when the materials are limited, but to be satisfied with a moderate height, combined with the avoidance of meagreness. In the genuine old romanesque spire there is every degree, from the pyramidal roof to considerable acuteness, but the usual tendency is to treat the spire as nothing more than a steep roof. In M. Dauvergne's church the spire is sharper, and the tower proportionately thinner than in the church of Notre Dame du Port, at Clermont, which is supposed to have been his model. The roof of the church itself is steeper, too, than was usually the genuine romanesque roof.* There is some reason to be apprehensive that the desire of the modern clergy, and the admiration of the modern laity, for mere height may lead to an adaptation of romanesque architecture to the tastes of the present day which would be foreign to its true spirit.

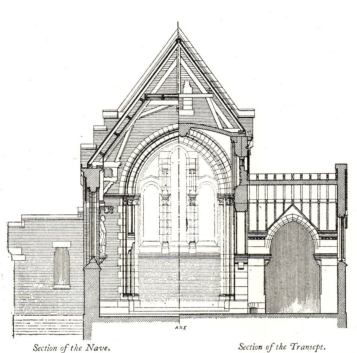

Section of the Nave.   *Section of the Transept.*

CHURCH AT SOUVERAIN-MOULIN.
M. E. Duthoit, Architect.

In the great romanesque church now in course of construction on the hill of Montmartre the modern desire for height would be unsatisfied were it not for the proposed dome and campanile, as yet existing only in the design of the architect. The first impression one receives on reaching the top of the long Montmartre stairs is disappointing. Having heard of the numerous millions of francs that have been already expended, we think there is little to show for the money. After visiting the interior, especially the crypt with its many and large chapels, we begin to understand that the building of the church has been like casting money into a coal-pit, a simile which the reader will see to be just when he learns that the massive piers on which the church is built are in more than eighty pits, each more than a hundred feet deep, and that the work of the foundations alone cost 200,000*l*. It is satisfactory to think that an architectural undertaking on a scale so colossal has been conducted on principles both of sound art and of common sense. Out of seventy-eight plans presented, the jury selected one that has the double advantage of recalling the old twelfth-century chapel of Montmartre, and of perpetuating the style to a very remote future by its almost incalculable durability. Had the style selected been, let us say, the Gothic of Beauvais, it would have

---

* When the cathedral at Autun was restored in the present century, an important part of the restoration consisted in removing a comparatively recent high-pitched roof to make room for a much lower one with the angle of the original romanesque. The improvement added greatly to the harmony of the edifice.

needed successive restorations; but unless this edifice is wilfully destroyed by enemies, it may last like the Pyramids. The present state of the building shows, in the interior, its enormous strength, but not its future splendour. One is impressed by the great vaults, by the wide span of the round arches under the dome, by the strength of the piers; but there is also an impression of nudity, darkness, and plainness. The darkness will be relieved by the light from the dome, the nudity and simplicity by mosaics, especially in the huge waggon-vault of the apse, whilst no doubt the impression of sublimity will be much enhanced by the height under the dome, now closed by a temporary roof. The severe simplicity of the exterior will be relieved by four minor domes, still important, and by many turrets with little domes, whilst the campanile will have a dome-roof carried high on a circular colonnade. If, as is probable, the necessary number of millions are forthcoming, the church of the Sacred Heart will be the most important ecclesiastical edifice constructed in Christendom since St. Paul's, and though not comparable for fecundity of invention to the best of the Gothic cathedrals, it will excel most of them in unity and severity of design, as well as in strength and durability. The domes and campanile will be the crown of Paris, visible from many a street in the city, as well as from all the country round. The names of serious architects are seldom popular, so it is not probable that M. Abadie, the designer of the Montmartre church, will rival the notoriety of M. Eiffel.

HOTEL DE VILLE AT LA FERTÉ-SOUS-JOUARRE.
M. P. Héneux, Architect.

The name of M. Eiffel reminds me that in France, during the last fifteen years, some attempts have been made to give to iron architecture artistic qualities, or, rather, to develop the artistic possibilities that may be inherent in the material. A powerful testimony in favour of iron was that of M. Viollet-le-Duc, whose knowledge of the older French architecture was unrivalled, so that his hopefulness for the new could never be said to proceed from ignorance. He hoped and believed that a new iron architecture would in course of time develop itself, and that it would be worthy of the nation that had produced the cathedrals of Rouen and Rheims. Certainly a great step has been made in this direction already. Viollet-le-Duc took the keenest interest in the buildings for the Exhibition of 1878. Had he lived till 1889 he would have seen great progress in the use of the new materials. I leave the Eiffel Tower out of the question. It is entirely engineer's work—an engineer's solution of the problem how to build the highest structure that will resist a hurricane with a very limited sum of money—and it is said by competent men that the problem cannot be solved in any form differing widely from that adopted by M. Eiffel. In a word, he did not choose his lines; they were imposed upon him by a scientific necessity. In architecture of a purely artistic kind the submission to scientific necessities is limited merely to a certain degree of stability and durability. Artistic design, to satisfy the eye and the mind, often goes quite outside of science—as, for example,

Y

in making parts of a building stronger than is necessary that the eye may not receive an impression, though a false impression, of weakness. In making artistic furniture, the supports for a light yet voluminous superstructure will be made thicker than necessary to support the *weight*, because the eye wants to have them thick to carry the visible *mass*. The main difficulty of iron architecture, and still more of steel, lies in the strength of the material. It is said that not a particle of iron, or wood either, has hitherto been admitted into the church of the Sacred Heart, so that building may be harmonious in its own way. An interesting and partially successful attempt was made to combine iron with stone in the

GALLERY AND LIBRARY AT TOULON.
M. G. Allar, Architect.

church of St. Augustine. A much more successful combination is that of iron with terra-cotta and *faïence* in the buildings of the last Universal Exhibition. The central dome, that of the Galerie de Trente Mètres, is too heavily charged with ornament on the outside ; the interior, however, is beautiful and worth preserving. But the most successful of all attempts in this most modern style of architecture are the two domes of the lateral buildings, the Palais des Beaux Arts and the Palais des Arts Libéraux. I have very frequently revisited that [of the Palais des Beaux Arts, and have each time been impressed, especially in the interior, by its structural elegance and its grace of proportion. The architect, M. Formigé, had cultivated a taste for elegance as architect of the promenades of Paris. If his work in the Champ de Mars is not more famous for architectural merit it is simply because it is near to us, and new, and connected with an industrial exhibition. It lacks the poetry that belongs, for us, to some 'Emir's dome' in the far East.

In public buildings other than ecclesiastical, there has been much employment for French architects since the establishment of the Republic. Great numbers of schools have been erected all over the country, and although these are chiefly of a utilitarian character, the objects being good light and air, and healthy accommodation rather than beauty, still many of the best architects in the provinces have done what they could to make school-buildings acceptable. I may mention M. Paugoy of Marseilles, and M. André of Lyons, as architects of good plain commercial schools, and M. Debaudeau of Paris as the architect of a more ambitious educational building, the Lycée Lakanal at Sceaux (seven miles from Paris), where, at a cost of about 500,000*l*., he succeeded in making what, according to French ideas, is a model public school for eight hundred boys of the middle classes. The Lycée Lakanal (which I have visited repeatedly and know in detail) is full of air and light, with most spacious halls, corridors, and class-rooms. The architecture can only be described as the most recent French, in which various materials — stone, iron, and bricks of different colours — are used with great liberty and originality. As this school is in the country, with wide grounds of its own, the architect has been free to do what was impossible in the old Parisian schools — spread his work out in distinct masses of building. Thus, the infirmary, the chapel, and some of the scientific class-rooms, as well as the gymnasium, are in the grounds, and the healthiness of the place may be understood from an answer made to me by a sister of charity in the infirmary. I praised the completeness of the appliances. 'Yes,' she said, 'we have everything here except patients.'

Many new town-halls have been erected in France during the last twenty years. I say nothing of the Parisian Hôtel de Ville, having described it in another work, and also because, though almost all its details are freshly invented, the general plan of it is copied from the old building, burnt in 1871. Some of the small provincial town-halls are very interesting. One of the best of them is that erected by M. Héneux at La Ferté-sous-Jouarre. With its broad stair ascending under the porch, its handsome windows and balcony, and its high-pitched roof crowned with a clock-turret, this building produces quite an imposing effect in the public place of the little town. The interior, too, presents a good deal of well-designed and interesting detail, including some good carving in wood and stone, and some artistic wrought ironwork.

An edifice of greater importance, in a style of architecture that recalls Italian predecessors more than French, is the combined gallery and library at Toulon by M. Allar. The accompanying illustration shows one of its richest and most picturesque corners, where the effects of light and shade must be superbly beautiful in the glaring sunshine of the south. Architecture such as this is too noble to be associated with the costumes of modern burgesses or tourists; it would need as an accompaniment the stately draperies of Paul Veronese.

Amongst recent museums I cannot omit the Musée Guimet at Paris, which contains objects illustrating the history of religions, and the Musée Galliéra, very near it, which

A SMALL HOUSE.
M. Deverin, *Architect.*

will contain nobody knows what. The Guimet Museum consists of two blocks of buildings independently designed, and each with a pediment in the middle. They stand back to back where two streets converge and almost join together at an angle where a circular structure occupies the corner. The idea was not a very happy one, nor was the site happily chosen, especially because there happened to be a block of houses showing an unfinished inner wall that the Museum does not hide, whilst it effectually prevents new houses from being built up to it. The Museum itself is an awkward structure, betraying great dearth of invention. The Musée Galliéra, on the other hand, by M. Ginain, is an exquisitely beautiful architectural composition, in a rich Renaissance, against which the only objection is that it can never afford an internal space answering to the outlay. It seems like an architect's fancy built for its own beauty. It is as yet unfinished, but will unquestionably be one of the best ornaments of Paris, admirably situated, too, with its own green lawn and enclosure.

I have said elsewhere that the modern French do not employ Gothic for their large tenement houses, finding, no doubt, the modern Parisian style more convenient. There are now, however, a considerable number of private houses which perpetuate the styles of French architecture prevalent in the fourteenth and fifteenth centuries. Some of these are extremely rich—for example, that by M. Février in the Place Malesherbes; but I have preferred

A HOUSE IN THE RUE DUMONT-DURVILLE.
M. Gaillard, Architect.

to take as an illustration a much smaller and plainer house by M. Deverin, which seems to me admirably consistent and tasteful in design. Again, not having much to say in favour of the way in which the Musée Guimet occupies the angle of two streets, I give one of the many favourable examples to be found in Paris where the difficulty is happily overcome. This is a charming house in the French Renaissance occupying an angle in the Rue Dumont-Durville. The architect is M. Gaillard, and his design is, I think, distinguished by great taste and judgment. I would invite the reader especially to notice the wise reserve in the use of ornament, the relief given by plain spaces, and the delicate quality of the ornamental sculpture which the architect has admitted.

I cannot conclude this imperfect notice of recent French architecture without thanking M. Ducher, the architectural publisher, for the assistance he has afforded in materials and illustration. His publications, especially 'Etudes de Façades, Maisons, Villas, Hôtels,' and the invaluable series of 'Monographies de Bâtiments Modernes,' by M. Raguenet, are of the greatest use to the student of modern French work in architecture. It is well known to every one who cares for architecture at all that careful and exact drawings make clearer to us even a building that we think we know quite intimately.

XII

Engraving, &c.

THE severity of the French system of art instruction, founded as it is on a serious discipline in drawing, must of itself tend to produce a good school of engravers, but the superior attractions of painting, and especially its lucrativeness in all cases of decided success, have withdrawn many of the best draughtsmen from engraving. The difference between the two professions is that, in painting, a very clever practitioner—such, for example, as M. Carolus Duran—can produce a satisfactory result in a very short time, whilst all engraving with the burin inexorably demands its count of days with so many hours of steady work in each of them. Etching appeared at first to come as a deliverance from this toil, but etching itself as time went on became a slavery too, as greater degrees of finish and more perfect tone were exacted from etchers by the publishers, and applauded by painters whose works were reproduced. One man of genius, Waltner, has indeed made a fortune by his rare skill in the use of etching and other rapid methods of engraving. I remember admiring, in his presence, the fine quality of certain tones in the background of a large portrait, and also in the dress and hair. 'Oh! that was an experiment,' he said; 'I got that quality with a file.' It is admitted, however, that Waltner may do what he likes. The commercial demand has its influence, rather, on inferior men who try to satisfy the trade. The consequence of the introduction of etching has been to increase immensely the number of these inferior men. The process of etching tempts by an apparent facility; it is at least much nearer to painting than the rigorous art of the burin: so that hundreds of artists, who would paint exclusively if they could sell pictures regularly, turn to etching that they may live without abandoning art. An eminent French painter said to me, 'In the last generation there were a dozen engravers in Paris; now there are several hundreds, and in this multitude there are but few thoroughly good draughtsmen.' The ordinary etcher often attains to a superficial imitation of texture and style, he very rarely acquires the power of first-rate draughtsmanship. The superiority of Flameng, who, though still working with undiminished ability, is already an ancestor in the history of Parisian engraving, is due to his thorough knowledge of drawing. This knowledge might be more general if a school of severe engraving could be maintained against the rivalry of photogravure, and a very earnest attempt is now being made to do this; but there is not a natural and popular demand for excellent engraving—there is only the encouragement of a small class of lovers of art inspired by a sense of duty. It may be doubted whether this will be sufficient to keep the art alive. There are, however, several examples of arts that are maintained without a natural demand, either by Governmental or other patronage—that is, by paying for what is not really wanted merely from a sense of duty to art. Engraving seems to be poorly aided by the State in France in comparison with sculpture. I am told that the Government spends 2400*l.* a year on the encouragement of engraving. There is the 'Chalcographie du Louvre,' a print-publishing establishment in the Louvre itself, that issues engravings from the works in the national collection at low prices. The quality of these plates varies very much. Some of them are of first-rate excellence, as, for example, the *Anne of Cleves* by Didier, after Holbein, and the *Portrait d'Homme* by Emile Rousseaux, after Francia; but these are not recent works, and so lie outside of my present subject. I

z

only wish to draw the reader's attention to the 'Chalcographie du Louvre' if he cares about serious engraving. A 'Société Française de Gravure' was founded in 1868, and it has since issued a certain number of good plates. The object of the founders was to keep the art alive by ensuring a sale for two engravings in the year. Lastly, we have the 'Société des Graveurs au Burin,' recently founded, and including the best line-engravers amongst its members. Here I must beg leave to offer a word of personal explanation. Notwithstanding three long visits to Paris in twelve months, it so happens, very unfortunately, that I have missed the exhibition of this Society, which had a special interest for me, and the only work exhibited there of which I have any right to speak is the engraving by M. Adrien Didier of *The Three Graces*, by Raphael, which was also exhibited at the Salon. This work is published this year (1891) by the Society, and may be taken as the representative example of the present state of burin-engraving in France. The picture is the well-known little work in the collection of the Duke of Aumale, for which that princely lover of art, whose enthusiasm does not cool with age, gave the magnificent sum of twenty-four thousand pounds. The engraving is the size of the original, and is, no doubt, extremely faithful; but fidelity in the sense of accurate copyism would not, of itself, ensure any eminent rank to an engraving. What is rare in this work of M. Didier is the completely sustained perfection of its technical style as an interpretation, by the burin, of just that kind of painting that the burin is able to interpret. I cannot at present call to mind any example of a *picture* by Raphael that has been better engraved. The plates after Raphael by the great Italian engravers were interpretations of his designs into an art severe and noble in itself, but taking no account of the qualities of painting. Now, in this work of M. Didier, the qualities of Raphael's early paintings, the modelling of the figures, the tone and texture of the landscape background, are followed with an affectionate and respectful exactness, which is truly remarkable when we remember the difficult and unaccommodating nature of the burin. However, as I have just said, there is sufficient affinity between this kind of painting and burin-engraving for such translation to be possible, nor has M. Didier in any way sacrificed the qualities of his own instrument to imitate those of the brush. His work is exquisitely right in all ways.*

A direct consequence of photographic engraving has been the tendency, in the most recent etching and dry-point work, to make the lines invisible by their very multiplicity, and effective only by tone and texture. One of the most favourable examples of this kind of work was a plate by M. Jeannin, after J. Gigoux, entitled *Rêverie*. This was published in 'L'Art' (vol. i., p. 105), and no doubt is a wonderful specimen of technical ability, if only because the artist was deprived of expressional powers which are very valuable in etching, and that few etchers would be willing to do without. A French engraver once told me that the present demand for etched work by publishers required a rivalry with photogravure, and that the object of the younger etchers was to equal photogravure in the perfection of tone along with invisibility of hand-work. I need hardly observe that nothing can be more opposed to the spirit of free linear etching, and the question naturally suggests itself, 'Why not get the picture reproduced by photogravure at once?' There is, however, an intermediate kind of work in which the lines, though extremely numerous, are still important, and which greatly excels photogravure, both in the transparence of shade and in the brilliance and purity of its lights. For example, our plate by M. Manesse, after the picture by Henry Lerolle, of *The Shepherds at Bethlehem*, is certainly far superior to photogravure in these respects and received the warm approval of the painter, and though the multiplicity of the lines makes them almost

---

* The number of impressions printed from the plates issued by the 'Société des Graveurs au Burin' is extremely limited, and the plates are afterwards destroyed. It is therefore impossible for us to give an example of their work otherwise than by one of the reproductive processes, which would not answer the purpose when perfection of technical quality is in question. There is another Society called 'La Société des Amis des Arts,' which to some extent encourages burin-engraving of the best quality.

H. Lerolle pinxit

Printed by Chardon Wittmann, Paris

Th. Hamerton sc.

THE SHEPHERDS AT BETHLEHEM

invisible at a little distance, still, if the reader will take the trouble to examine them closely, he will see that the direction of all of them has been very carefully determined, and that they are not thrown in indiscriminately, as they are in inferior work. This plate, by the way, may stand as a sufficient answer to the assertion that truth of shade cannot be obtained in etching. The result, too, was not obtained in a slow and tentative manner; the elaborate linear work was on the plate before it was first bitten. I saw it there.*

The present state of engravers' etching in Paris may be estimated accurately by the plates issued in 'L'Art' and THE PORTFOLIO, except that these periodicals cannot publish plates of very large dimensions, such as those which are exhibited, for the purpose of winning reputation, in the Salon. M. Manesse, for example, set himself to rival the great engravers of the eighteenth century in his fine large portrait of the Archbishop of Rouen, for which the Archbishop gave sittings, as to a painter, and the plate was unquestionably a success. M. Leopold Flameng does not belong to the present generation of engravers, who look up to him as the father of modern picturesque engraving in France, but his large portrait of Shakespeare was exhibited in the Salon of 1891. It is from the Chandos picture, which does not, in reality, contain enough material to supply all that a great engraver wants, so that M. Flameng's work, without departing from the original in the matter of likeness, contains a good deal of original invention or induction. I mean that when an artist as learned as M. Flameng has to make something out of a work that is not learned, his own knowledge enables him to make inferences from the meagre and insufficient material. A more straightforward, if less stimulating task, is the interpretation of a work that supplies material in abundance, like the large mural painting of *The Death of St. Geneviève*, by Jean Paul Laurens, in the Pantheon, which M. Flameng has engraved on a large scale, and with the most laborious care and fidelity. Another veteran, M. Brunet-Debaines, exhibited a large etching, after Keeley Halswelle, from the landscape entitled *Willows whiten, Aspens quiver*. The subject is a pond with a mass of trees reflected in the middle, and on the surface an abundance of flowering aquatic plants. The plate displayed great mastery, both of art and nature.

Amongst newer names of etchers who work from pictures I may mention M. Eugène Fornet, who interprets Henner with great fidelity, suggesting admirably the painter's qualities of execution. J. Torné contributed two of the best etchings to the forty-fifth volume of 'L'Art.' Daniel Mordant has etched good plates after Goya ('L'Art,' xliii., 58), and Ulysse Butin ('L'Art,' xlii., 40). E. Daumont contributed to one of these volumes an April landscape after Zuber, a river scene remarkable for its truth of pale tones, but weak, though delicate, in drawing. P. Lafond has interpreted Charles Jacque almost as well as that skilful painter-etcher could interpret his own work, and much in his manner. A. Masson has a hard and clear style of engraving, suitable for certain pictures, but which he modifies when working, for example, after Ribot. All these are accomplished men, and if I do not extend the list it is because laconic criticism is unreadable, and I have not space for more.

At the time of the revival of etching—that is, from 1858 to 1868—I had hoped, along with a few others, that original engraving would take its place by the side of original painting, and that there would be a fertile production of really autographic work on copper. Unfortunately, the art of picturesque engraving has been employed almost exclusively in the

---

* The picture by M. Lerolle, from which this work is engraved, may be taken as an excellent example of the best modern realism in the treatment of sacred subjects. The reader will see for himself that, although the painter has entirely discarded all the decorative enrichments with which mediaeval artists adorned subjects of this kind, and has not cared for the dignity of attitude and gesture which the painters of the Renaissance substituted for mediaeval jewellery, still, his realism is very remote from that vulgar realism which rejoices in depreciating noble subjects. M. Lerolle's mural pictures (St. Martin and others) are proof enough that his conception of art rises far above the commonplace.

interpretation of painting. However, there are still a few original etchers in France, some of them very skilful. There is M. Edmond Yon, whose variously accomplished hand turns from painting to etching, and from etching to wood-engraving without betraying the amateur in either. M. Ardail, a highly-trained pupil of Waltner, produces original etchings, as, for example, his fine and truthful portrait of President Carnot, which is the frontispiece to the fiftieth volume of 'L'Art,' and on which no labour has been wasted. M. Lepère, whose painted landscapes I have noticed, is a clever original etcher and wood-engraver. His etchings, which are linear and intentionally very slight in treatment, leave much more white paper than is usual in etchings from pictures. They can scarcely be said to be published, as a very few copies are printed of each before the plate is destroyed, and the artist himself looks upon them chiefly as free experiments in an art that interests him. After watching very carefully the effects of the revival of etching in England and France for the last thirty years, I have come to the conclusion that the qualities that at first attracted us in the free etchings of painters, and which, after all, are really what we call the qualities of etching, are best attained, if ever, by an accomplished painter who takes to copper in a mood of affectionate recreation. M. Lepère told me that nothing had ever interested him so much as etching, because thought expressed itself so quickly by the process, whilst there was so little technical hindrance. The last reason would not be given by an etcher from pictures.

If the etchings of M. Lepère are linear, in wood-engraving he works, within fixed limits, for tone. There was an interesting woodcut by him—I mean an original—in one of the exhibitions, representing the space before the Houses of Parliament at Westminster. It was extremely clever, though wood-engraving is hardly adapted to the expression of original thought, except on the understanding that the artist is to copy some design that he has already made in a more tractable material. M. Lepère is, however, not the only contemporary French artist who does original work on wood. M. Farlet engraved a subject of his own invention entitled, *Que fait-elle ?* Three children are together in the country ; the elder girl is seeking for something in a bush, the little ones look on curiously—that is all ; but for skill in minute engraving this woodcut has seldom been equalled. The clearness and abundance of detail, and the painstaking fidelity to nature, remind one of principles that were prevalent in the English school thirty or forty years ago. The versatility of wood-engraving in the interpretation of other arts has been proved abundantly by the Americans. The French seem to be trying its powers now in very various directions. M. Duplessis, in an engraving from a picture entitled *Quiétude*, by Duffaut, seems to have aimed at the qualities of etching ; M. Maurand, in *The Old Dwelling*, after Lhermitte, has imitated the quality of Lhermitte's charcoal drawings, whilst Mlle. Juliette Leluc, in her wood-engraving of the *Danse des Bacchantes*, by Corot, has rendered the tender quality of Corot's painting so marvellously, that I doubt if I have ever seen it so exactly rendered before in any kind of art. The possible rivalry of wood with steel or copper seems almost proved by an astonishing woodcut by M. Emile Derbier after a *Judith and Holophernes*, by Cranach : the combined delicacy and clearness of this work, the sureness of hand and eye required for its execution, are enough to rivet the attention of any one who knows what engraving is. How it would have astonished Dürer—I mean as evidence of modern technical progress in wood-engraving. M. Félix Jasinski, a Pole naturalised in France, displays great skill and knowledge of the old masters in two engravings after Dürer and Botticelli. Surely work of this fine quality deserves quite as much honour as if it had been done on copper.

The tradition of original work has not been entirely lost even in lithography, an art that has long remained out of fashion, and that can hardly make much way, in these times, against the facilities of drawing on paper for reproduction by photogravure. There are still good lithographers in France, and I noticed with interest that in the Salon of 1891 nine or ten of them exhibited original works, and took care to describe them as original in the catalogue. This is as it should be, for whenever an art has been entirely given over to the copyist, it has invariably declined. Amongst the original lithographs in the Salon were some studies of wild beasts by M. Adolphe Millot, including a lion which was admirable. His portraits seemed to me less admirable, being hard and too clearly detailed, as well as on too small a scale. One of the best qualities of lithography is its richness—what the French call its fatness—and the endeavour to give it the hard precision that belongs to line-engraving robs it of this quality. The finest lithographs have been broadly and rather bluntly drawn, with full darks and on rather large stones.

A class of artists who do not usually excite any keen public interest, and yet who frequently deserve it by their patient labour and accomplished skill, are the medal and gem engravers. Every Englishman who takes an interest in the fine arts knows the leading French painters and sculptors of statues, but he is not likely to know the names of those wonderful workers in little who cut the cornelian or the sardonyx. Yet their labours may outlast not only our iron towers and bridges, but the most valued of large works in the fine arts. The time may come when the gems we so easily overlook will be the representatives of the French art of to-day. To estimate these minute and exquisite works at their true value, we ought to have a special and peculiar interest in them—and this, I fear, is often wanting. Considering the extreme inconvenience of large works of art in small Parisian apartments, and the handsome incomes of many people who are very narrowly lodged, it seems as if no place could be more favourable than the Paris of to-day for the encouragement of an art that produces objects so beautiful, so portable, and so precious. Very few artists of any kind have attained the union of qualities that we call *perfection* so completely as Louis Roty, the medal engraver. There is, for example, the portrait-plaquette of M. Hirn, as good as a drawing by Holbein; the medal of Sir John Pope Hennessy, the medal of Mounet-Sully, the well-known tragedian, besides *plaquettes*, such as that of the French Alpine Club, all of consummate excellence in a style at once severe and full of character. It is interesting to observe how rapidly new things gain a place for themselves in the fine arts. The bicycle has only been current (*current* indeed!) during a few years, but we have it already in a large medal by M. Dubois, and it does really very well as a subject of art, aided as it is by the neat costumes of the riders, which display the human figure to great advantage, and permit the full expression of muscular strength or agility. As medals are given for prizes in athletic contests, M. Lavée has enjoyed a good opportunity with his subject of runners arriving at the goal. Agriculture, too, offers available subjects with the necessary degree of simplification and idealisation; and agriculture in France is more than ever held in honour now that it has an Order of Merit of its own. Every year the features of President Carnot and a few other political celebrities are immortalised afresh in medals and medallions, whilst the tendency to that kind of portraiture for people in more private stations appears to be on the increase. The art, then, is not without that contact with contemporary reality which is necessary to the health and vigour of every fine art. Still, it has not abandoned either the historic past or the poetic ideal. M. Lemaire recurs to the tale of Orpheus and Eurydice. M. Mouchon also goes back to Orpheus. The interest of the old legends is not yet exhausted.

Here may end a survey of the present state of the fine arts in France, which I do not offer as without omissions, but which will, at least, have given a truthful idea of the different tendencies most prevalent in the French school. It may be considered an omission not to have dwelt more particularly on water-colour and on pastel; but the truth is, that the essential differences between those arts and oil-painting may be described in a very few words, and that the artistic tendencies of an epoch are exactly the same whether they manifest themselves in one medium or another. In water-colour and pastel the modern Frenchman seeks, above all things, for freshness; I mean that he dislikes laboured work, and tries, at least, to make his drawings appear as if they were not laboured, but the direct expression of his thought.   If this tendency were peculiar to water-colour, then that art would have a special interest of its own ; but, in fact, we find it equally in much contemporary oil-painting.   All these arts are practised by the same men.   The oil-painter turns to water-colour or pastel for a variety or for his convenience in study ; if he is a landscape-painter he has probably used water-colour for his sketches from nature, and the transition to making a water-colour for exhibition is not like taking up a new art. M. Lhermitte works in pastel after working much in charcoal and in oil.   Is it not easy to see that the technical accomplishment of the pastellist was ready to his hand, that the handling of charcoal and pastel are almost the same, and that the drawing came from charcoal and the colour from oil?   The catalogue of the 'Société des Pastellistes' contains quite a list of names already well known amongst painters.   In 1889 the deceased members were Baudry, Boulanger, Rousseau, Guillaumet—all painters ; and the members who had resigned were Clairin, Jacquet, Rafaelli, and Vollon—all painters again.   The names in the catalogue of active contributors included such well-known painters as Adan, Béraud, Besnard, John-Lewi, Brown, Cazin, Dagnan - Bouveret, Dubufe, Duez, François Flameng, Heilbuth, Lefebvre, Madeleine-Lemaire, Lévy, Lhermitte, Montenard, Moreau, Nozal, Puvis de Chavannes, Roll, Tissot, Yon. I may, therefore, be pardoned for not expatiating separately on their merits as pastellists, which are exactly the same as their merits in the art of painting, the art that taught them all they know and all that they express in pastel with greater manual facility.

My general conclusion from this survey of contemporary French art is, that there is no lack of vitality in it, but that the invasion of modern realism has destroyed all authority whatever.   The French school is, in fact, in a condition of the most complete anarchy, and is no more a school in the sense of any common purpose than the business association of individual artists in England can constitute a school.   In a word, the condition of French artists to-day is that of perfect freedom for individual talents and of surprising independence as regards the past.   This will be seen very plainly when, after the lapse of a few years, some of the most modern of modern pictures find their way into the Louvre.

London : Printed by STRANGEWAYS AND SONS Tower Street, Cambridge Circus, W.C.

Price 21*s. Cloth, Large Medium* 8*vo.*
Large Paper Edition (100 *only*) 42*s.*

THE LIFE AND LETTERS OF
SAMUEL PALMER

PAINTER AND ETCHER

Written and Edited by A. H. PALMER

WITH NINE COPPER-PLATES AND OTHER ILLUSTRATIONS

Price 21*s. Cloth*

AN ENGLISH VERSION OF
THE ECLOGUES

OF

VIRGIL

By SAMUEL PALMER

SECOND EDITION

WITH ILLUSTRATIONS BY THE AUTHOR

Price 21*s. Cloth*

THE MINOR POEMS

OF

JOHN MILTON

WITH TWELVE ILLUSTRATIONS

By SAMUEL PALMER

PAINTER AND ETCHER

London : SEELEY & Co. LIMITED, Essex Street, Strand

Price 21s. Cloth

THE BRITISH SEAS

By W. CLARK RUSSELL

AND OTHERS

*ILLUSTRATED WITH ETCHINGS AND VIGNETTES AFTER MANY
WELL-KNOWN MARINE PAINTERS*

Price 21s. Cloth

WESTMINSTER ABBEY

By W. J. LOFTIE

WITH MANY ILLUSTRATIONS BY HERBERT RAILTON

Price 21s. Cloth

THE LAUREATE'S COUNTRY

A DESCRIPTION OF PLACES CONNECTED WITH
THE LIFE OF ALFRED LORD TENNYSON

By A. J. CHURCH, M.A.

WITH MANY ILLUSTRATIONS FROM DRAWINGS BY EDWARD HULL

London: SEELEY & Co. LIMITED, Essex Street, Strand